THE
STOOGEPHILE
TRIVIA
BOOK

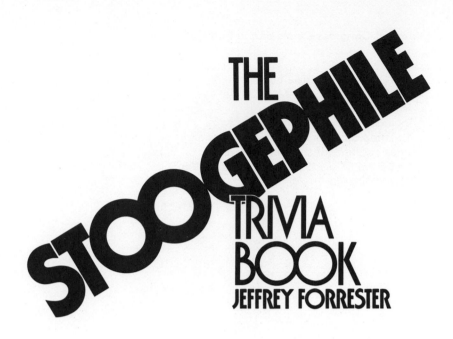

THE STOOGEPHILE TRIVIA BOOK

JEFFREY FORRESTER

RESEARCH CONSULTANT:
STEPHEN COX

ILLUSTRATOR:
TOM HANSEN

Contemporary Books, Inc.
Chicago

Library of Congress Cataloging in Publication Data

Forrester, Jeffrey.
    The Stoogephile trivia book.

    Filmography: p.
    Includes index.
    1. Three Stooges movies—Miscellanea.   2. Three
Stooges (Comedy team)—Miscellanea.   I. Title.
PN1995.9.T5F67   1982   791.43'028'0922   82-45435
ISBN 0-8092-5613-4

Published by Contemporary Books, Inc.
180 North Michigan Avenue, Chicago, Illinois 60601
Manufactured in the United States of America
Library of Congress Catalog Card Number: 82-45435
International Standard Book Number: 0-8092-5613-4

Published simultaneously in Canada by
Beaverbooks, Ltd.
150 Lesmill Road
Don Mills, Ontario M3B 2T5
Canada

CONTENTS

Foreword   v

Preface   ix

Acknowledgments   xi

Introduction   xiii

1   THE MEN BEHIND THE MAYHEM   1

2   THE ART OF ARTLESSNESS   49

3   A LEGACY OF LAUGHTER   85

Appendix: Three Stooges Filmography   107

Index   125

FOREWORD

I'm crazy about the Three Stooges. I admired them in the late 1950s, when their old two-reel comedies began popping up on television, a development that launched Curly, Larry, Moe, and Shemp on a second life of runaway popularity. And I like them even more today, as their raucous, histrionic routines continue to get pumped into millions of homes via local stations and cable companies.

No, I don't possess that smug superiority that many people use against the Stooges—as if the boys' antics are beneath the dignity of an intelligent, mature adult—and I don't fear that children might be transformed into violent bullies because of their fascination with the legendary comedy trio.

Does that make me irresponsible? Am I slipping into a second childhood already?

Or is there more to the Stooges than the repetitious sights of Moe whacking Curly, Shemp, or Larry over the head with a mallet, tweaking their noses, gouging their eyes, kicking them in the shins, slapping them across the face, and using their skulls to test a buzz saw?

On the 50th anniversary of the formation of the Three Stooges an increasing number of observers are admitting that the boys were vastly underrated throughout their careers. Indeed, America's favorite Stooge, Jerry "Curly" Howard, must have been the most underappreciated funnyman of his day. Thoroughly unsung by the critics and opinion makers during his 1934–46 stint with the Stooges, Curly nevertheless probably triggered more man-hours of laughter than any other comic of that era.

For kids, Curly was a natural. The dozens of bits of physical shtick, the high-pitched prissy voice, and that wonderfully ingratiating personality made this man-child a favorite of youngsters everywhere. But to look at Curly from an adult standpoint is to realize that there was a lot more to that fat, shaved-headed clown than the plaintive cry of "Moe! Larry! Cheese!"

No, Curly Howard was a uniquely graceful comic performer. Despite his considerable girth, he glided across a dance floor, he could walk or run in almost poetic synch with his dialogue, and he invented some of the most uproarious military marching routines on film. He also played that absurd, cackling voice like a fine musical instrument.

Despite their specialty of low-rent, roughhouse comedy, the Three Stooges were solid, dependable workmen who occasionally scaled extraordinary artistic heights. Considering the comparatively tiny budgets they were forced to work with for 25 years at Columbia Pictures, their on-screen achievements are nothing short of remarkable.

Even though the boys were continually hounded by a Hollywood caste system that pigeonholed them as "second rate," Curly, Larry, Moe, and Shemp have withstood the test of time handsomely. Long after their deaths, they still hold an amazing grip on the hearts and minds of millions of us, and as the 1980s roll by, it looks more like the Three Stooges finally are being recognized for what they were— the most skillful practitioners of farce-comedy ever to ply their trade in this country.

Gary Deeb
Syndicated TV Columnist
Chicago *Sun-Times*

John Candy as Curly. (Photo courtesy of John Candy.)

PREFACE

I was very flattered and honored when I was asked to write the preface to this book, until I learned there wasn't any money involved. Be that as it may, I find it hard to express in just a few lines what the Three Stooges have meant to me. Their influence on my work has been great, as watching an SCTV show will prove.

The Stooges are thought of by many as broad physical comics. To me the magic of their humor was their subtlety. Of course, the odd slap in the face or the two fingers in the eyes didn't hurt.

What can I say? The Three Stooges were great, and I miss them. My one regret is never having met them. Just once I would have liked to exit an office, turn, and say, "I'll be back in an hour . . . are you boys *sure* you know what you're doing?"

Enjoy the book!

John Candy
"SCTV Network"

ACKNOWLEDGMENTS

Special thanks to John Candy and Gary Deeb for their generous cooperation and contributions.

Thanks also to John A. Barbour and Jonathan L. Carbary for their assistance.

And, of course, thanks to the many people whose personal recollections provided the material for this book. It certainly would not have been possible without them.

INTRODUCTION

Exactly what is a Stoogephile?

According to the *American Heritage Dictionary of the English Language, -phile* means ". . . one having love or strong affinity or preference for . . ." Therefore, a *Stooge-phile* would be someone who has love or strong affinity or preference for a Stooge, or for Stooges.

On the basis of that definition, I am a Stoogephile. I was born the year after the old Three Stooges movies began running on television, and grew up watching them every weekday afternoon on a local TV station. And I'm not embarrassed to say that I watched them religiously all the way through grammar school, high school, and college.

The Three Stooges have always attracted a large audience; they made more films than any other comedy team in movie history. But it wasn't until recently that their popularity with adults grew to near-superstar proportions. The country has taken notice; in the last few years, Americans have been inundated with Three Stooges film festivals, television revivals, and, of course, Three Stooges merchandise.

A whole new generation of TV-bred kids are growing up enjoying the Stooges' fast-paced, slap-happy antics. So, Stoogemania continues to flourish. This book was written especially for Stoogemaniacs. A Stoogemaniac is, of course, a rabid Stoogephile.

Stoogephiles and Stoogemaniacs (myself included) are interested in each and every bit of trivia pertaining to the Stooges' career: Which films used footage from other films? Who played the role of the cop in this episode? Is this a "Shemp" short or a "Curly" short? Why did Curly shave his head in the first place? Who invented the "poke in the eyes"? Why did Curly retire?

The Stoogephile Trivia Book is intended to be both fun and informative, full of crucial information you can toss around at the next swanky society party you're invited to. Remember, though—you'll make a better impression by talking about the Stooges than by behaving like them. As a rule of thumb, 'tis better to toss trivia facts than custard pies.

But then again, as the Stooges themselves proved time after time, rules were made to be broken. . . .

Jeffrey Forrester

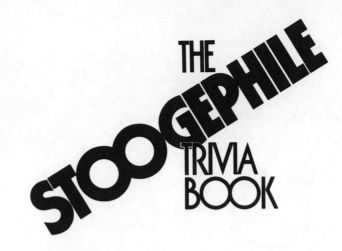

1
THE MEN BEHIND THE MAYHEM

VITAL STOOGETISTICS

No other comedy team in movie history amassed as many different members as the Three Stooges. Thanks to its generic name, the group could easily shuffle around personnel whenever necessary. When one of the Stooges died or simply dropped out a new member could always be brought in as a replacement. This, perhaps, was the secret of the team's longevity.

The mainstays of the ensemble were the Howard brothers: Moe, Curly, and Shemp. (The Howards had two other brothers, Jack and Irving, neither of whom pursued show business careers.) For a number of years two Howard brothers—either Moe and Curly or Moe and Shemp—comprised part of the group. But all three brothers never worked together as Stooges.

The Three Stooges started as part of a vaudeville act. The original members of the team had served as second bananas, or "stooges," to Ted Healy, a stand-up comedian. When "Ted Healy and His Stooges" broke up in the 1930s, the Stooges formed their own act, the "Three Stooges." It was later to become the most popular comedy team in the country.

Moe Howard
("The First Stooge")

★ *Real Name*	Harry Horwitz
★ *Year of Birth*	1897
★ *Year of Death*	1975
★ *Married*	Helen Schonberger (1925)
★ *Children*	Joan, Paul
★ *First Year of Stooging*	1925
★ *Last Year of Stooging*	1969
★ *Career Prior to the Three Stooges*	Began in silent movies as child actor. Also worked on showboats as dramatic actor. Eventually became vaudeville comedian.
★ *Hobbies*	Enjoyed gardening and making hooked rugs.
★ *Aversions*	Hated to be late for appointments.

Moe Howard joined "Ted Healy and His Stooges" in 1925. He served as "leader," or "First Stooge," of the trio from that point forward. After leaving Healy in the 1930s the Stooges lasted for more than three decades as an independent group under Moe's guidance. After establishing the Three Stooges, he acquired substantial real estate holdings, including a drugstore and an apartment building. He even owned his own furniture store, the Howard Furniture Company, of Burbank, California.

Moe Howard, the leader figure of the Stooges. (From the MGM release Dancing Lady *© 1933 Metro-Goldwyn-Mayer Corporation. Copyright renewed 1960 by Metro-Goldwyn-Mayer Inc.)*

Moe Howard has been described as both a very hard-working performer and a very sensitive individual. Says Stooges director Edward Bernds: "Moe was, of course, very touchy. But he was also a very, very dedicated performer. A lot of people have more or less commended me for something I did in the late 1950s, after the Stooges were dropped from Columbia. I was directing a science fiction picture, and I gave Moe a bit part as a taxi driver. Well, now everybody says, 'Gee, it sure was great of you to get Moe some work when he was down.' Moe wasn't down; he was a *millionaire!* But he really wanted to work; he really wanted to act. He was so dedicated to his profession that he would take a bit part in a feature film just to be acting again."

After a bout with cancer Moe Howard died in 1975, just weeks before his golden wedding anniversary.

Larry Fine
("The Second Stooge")

★ *Real Name*	**Louis Feinberg**
★ *Year of Birth*	**1902**
★ *Year of Death*	**1975**
★ *Married*	**Mabel Haney (1926)**
★ *Children*	**Phyllis, John**
★ *First Year of Stooging*	**1925**
★ *Last Year of Stooging*	**1969**

★ *Career Prior to the Three Stooges*	**Began with vaudeville singing act as a child. Later formed his own musical act. Eventually became vaudeville comedian.**
★ *Hobbies*	**Enjoyed owning large automobiles.**
★ *Aversions*	**Disliked long conferences.**

Larry Fine played the middleman, or "peacemaker," of the Three Stooges throughout the team's existence. He started out in vaudeville as a musician and played violin for a singing act called "Haney Sisters and Fine." So close was their working relationship that Larry even wound up marrying one of the sisters, Mabel Haney. While working with a musical act in Chicago in 1925 he was hired to join Ted Healy's Stooges. Larry remained with the Stooges until they disbanded in 1969.

Unlike Moe Howard, Larry Fine had little interest in the Stooges' business matters. The only business Larry concerned himself with was show business, despite the fact that he entered the jewelry trade as a very young man. Larry's father, Joseph Feinberg, owned a jewelry store, and Larry temporarily joined his dad's line of work. But Larry's clowning interfered with business, so the elder Feinberg gave his son a $100 bonus and two weeks' salary and asked him to quit. Larry obliged and subsequently became a vaudeville performer.

Years later, after Larry had suffered a stroke and was confined to a wheelchair, he spoke in a radio interview of his lack of interest in business. "We made a lot of money. Moe knew what to do with it—I spent it!"

Larry was a very easy-going fellow. In the late 1950s, Shemp Howard's widow, Babe Howard, attempted to sue

Larry Fine, the team's long-suffering middleman. (From the MGM release Dancing Lady © *1933 Metro-Goldwyn-Mayer Corporation. Copyright renewed 1960 by Metro-Goldwyn-Mayer Inc.)*

the "Three Stooges" for a percentage of their earnings. "Moe wouldn't speak to me," says Babe, "but Larry couldn't have cared less. In fact, I ran into him once and I was wearing a mink stole. He told me, 'By the time you get finished with us, you'll have *six* of those!' "

Larry often complained that he didn't like to sit through Three Stooges films, because he didn't like to watch himself. "I notice all the mistakes I made," he said. "But I guess everybody does that."

Larry Fine died of a stroke in 1975. At the time of his death he was a resident of the Motion Picture Country Home in Woodland Hills, California, a facility supported by the movie industry.

Curly Howard
("The Third Stooge")

★ *Real Name*	Jerome Horwitz
★ *Year of Birth*	1903
★ *Year of Death*	1952
★ *Married*	Valerie Neuman (1947). Also had one annulled marriage and two divorces prior to marrying Valerie Neuman.
★ *Children*	Marilyn (by previous marriage) Janie (by Valerie)

★ *First Year of Stooging*   1932

★ *Last Year of Stooging*   1946

★ *Career Prior to
the Three Stooges*   **Appeared as comedy conductor with band in vaudeville. Eventually became vaudeville comedian.**

★ *Hobbies*   **Enjoyed collecting dogs.**

★ *Aversions*   **Hated mistreatment of animals.**

Curly Howard played the patsy of the trio and is undoubtedly the most popular of all the various Stooges. He started out in show business as a comedy conductor with the Orville Knapp Band in vaudeville. When his older brother, Shemp, left Ted Healy's Stooges in the early 1930s Curly begged him to talk Healy into using him as a replacement. After joining the Stooges Curly quickly became the star of the group. He remained with the trio until ill health forced him into retirement in 1946.

Curly has been described by Stooges producer Jules White as "the life of the party." He was married several times; his first marriage, at age 17, was annulled by his mother, while a later marriage ended in divorce after only a few months. Curly was likable, fun-loving, and extremely generous. He was well liked by his fellow comedians. Curly was also a heavy drinker, and in 1945 he suffered a stroke at the age of 42. He continued to work with the Stooges, however, until his retirement in 1946. While relaxing on the set of **Half-Wits Holiday** (1947), his last film as one of the trio, Curly suffered a more damaging stroke and was forced to leave the Stooges. He did, however, return to make a cameo appearance in **Hold That Lion** (1947), a Stooges short subject featuring Shemp Howard.

Curly Howard, the lovable simpleton of the trio. (From the MGM release Beer and Pretzels © *1933 Metro-Goldwyn-Mayer Corporation. Copyright renewed 1960 by Metro-Goldwyn-Mayer Inc.)*

While recuperating in a rest home, Curly married a nurse, Valerie Neuman, and began a new family. In the next few years, however, he suffered several additional strokes. Curly died in 1952, when he was 49 years old.

Curly, as he appeared after his retirement, relaxes with his baby, Janie, and his wife, Valerie. (Photos courtesy of Jane Howard Hanky.)

Curly Howard, the family man.
(Photos courtesy of Jane Howard
Hanky.)

Shemp Howard

(replaced Curly Howard in 1946)

* **Real Name** — Sam Horwitz

* **Year of Birth** — 1895

* **Year of Death** — 1955

* **Married** — Gertrude "Babe" Frank (1925)

* **Children** — Morton

* **First Year of Stooging** — 1925

* **Last Year of Stooging** — 1955

* **Career Prior to the Three Stooges** — Began as comedian in vaudeville. Also appeared in short subjects and feature films as solo performer.

* **Hobbies** — Enjoyed watching prizefights.

* **Aversions** — Hated to get sick.

Shemp was the original member of the Stooges. He joined Ted Healy in 1925 and eventually brought in brother Moe and Larry Fine. Shemp dropped out of the Stooges trio in 1932 to pursue a solo career. He was replaced in the act by another brother, Curly. Shemp, who was starring in short subjects at Columbia Pictures, was forced to return to the Stooges in 1946 after Curly suffered a stroke, and he remained with the team until he suffered a heart attack in 1955.

Shemp has been described by many of those who worked with the Stooges—including director Edward Bernds, fellow

Shemp and Babe Howard at a family get-together in the late 1940s. (Photo courtesy of Babe Howard.)

performer Emil Sitka, and others—as the most "naturally funny" member of the group, as well as the most likable. Despite his gruff exterior, Shemp was a gentle and generous individual. For example, after his agent died in the 1940s Shemp continued to give a percentage of his movie salary to the agent's widow on a voluntary basis.

Shemp was less tough than the character he often played in movies; his widow, Babe Howard, characterized him as "afraid of everything." During the Second World War Babe served as an air raid warden. While she would make the rounds throughout the neighborhood, Shemp would stay home and hide behind the piano.

Shemp never even learned how to drive an automobile. Shemp's fear of driving resulted from a bad experience he had as a young man. While brother Moe was giving him a driving lesson, Shemp accidentally drove his car through a barbershop window! That was enough to convince him to leave the driving to others.

Shemp died of a heart attack in 1955, while riding in the back of a cab with some friends after attending a boxing match.

Joe Besser

(replaced Shemp Howard in 1956)

★ *Real Name*	Joseph Besser
★ *Year of Birth*	1907
★ *Year of Death*	
★ *Married*	Erna Kay (1932)
★ *Children*	None
★ *First Year of Stooging*	1956
★ *Last Year of Stooging*	1958

Joe Besser poses outside his home in the late 1970s. (Photo courtesy of Edward McCullough.)

★ **Career Prior to the Three Stooges**

Began with magic act in vaudeville. Later appeared as comedian in vaudeville and burlesque. Also appeared in short subjects, feature films, and on television as solo performer.

★ **Hobbies**

Enjoys repairing toys (for neighborhood children).

★ **Aversions**

Aggravated by demanding fans.

Joe Besser joined the Stooges after Shemp Howard died in 1955. Like Shemp, Joe Besser had starred in short subjects at Columbia Pictures. While under contract at Columbia, Joe was inducted as Shemp's replacement. Joe started out in show business as an assistant to magician Howard Thurston but later went solo. One of his many fans was Lou Costello, who later became half of one of the most popular comedy teams of all time, Abbott and Costello. Costello and Besser became close friends, and Joe says he was the only outsider invited to Costello's home for Christmas.

Joe left the Stooges in 1958 when the team was planning a nationwide personal appearance tour. Besser was already signed to appear as a solo performer in the film *Say One for Me* (1959) and was forced to drop out. Since leaving the Stooges Joe has made innumerable appearances and until recently was busy supplying voices for various Saturday morning cartoon shows.

Joe's wife, Ernie, was also in show business, as a dancer and choreographer. Today the Bessers live in the Los Angeles area.

Joe DeRita
(replaced Joe Besser in 1958)

★ *Real Name*   **Joseph Wardell**

★ *Year of Birth*   **1909**

★ *Year of Death*

★ *Married*   **Jean Sullivan**

★ *Children*	**None**
★ *First Year of Stooging*	**1958**
★ *Last Year of Stooging*	**1969**
★ *Career Prior to the Three Stooges*	**Began as part of dancing act in vaudeville. Later appeared as comedian in vaudeville and burlesque. Also appeared in short subjects and feature films as solo performer.**
★ *Hobbies*	**Enjoys watching sports.**
★ *Aversions*	**Dislikes rude people.**

Joe DeRita and wife Jean at home.
(Photo courtesy of Stephen Cox.)

Joe DeRita is the only Stooge whose parents were also in show business. He started on the stage at an early age, with his mother and sister in a dancing act called "DeRita Sisters and Junior." When he was a teenager Joe went out on his own with a solo comedy act.

Joe later became one of the biggest stars in the postwar years of burlesque. During the Second World War he entertained troops overseas, often using Bing Crosby as his straight man. After returning to the United States Joe joined Harold Minsky's burlesque outfit and quickly became Minsky's top banana comic. It was during his Minsky tenure that Joe DeRita came to the attention of the Three Stooges. They hired him as a replacement for Joe Besser, and he became the final Stooge recruit to make movies with the team. Like the two "replacement" Stooges before him, Joe also starred in short subjects at Columbia Pictures.

Joe is now retired and lives with his wife, Jean, in a suburb of Los Angeles.

THE RIGHT DIRECTION

Next to the Stooges themselves, the most important figure in the production of their short subjects was their director. The success or failure of each film depended heavily on the talent and experience of the man directly in charge—and in Columbia's Short Subjects Department this was the director.

Jules White

The Three Stooges might not have ever become starring film comedians had it not been for director/producer Jules White. For White was the man that hired them to make movies at Columbia in 1934, shortly after they had left Ted Healy. At that time White was head of the studio's shorts department. In fact, he had literally assembled the division several years earlier.

Jules White, holding a photo taken of himself in the 1930s, at home. The walls of White's study are covered with photos of comedy stars whose films he produced. (Photo courtesy of Edward McCullough.)

Under White's tutelage the Three Stooges series lasted a record-breaking 25 years. White himself directed the majority of their films and produced most of them as well. After 1952 the Stooges comedies became White's sole responsibility.

White was a vastly experienced director and producer prior to working with the Stooges. He had started out working for Mack Sennett, the king of silent comedy, as a gag writer. Eventually White became one of the most prolific directors in the short subject comedy business.

White, who retired in the early 1960s, was honored in 1982 by the Academy of Motion Picture Arts and Sciences for his contributions to screen comedy. A special celebration was held in his honor in Los Angeles, complete with screenings of some of his Three Stooges films. Altogether, White directed 104 Stooges shorts.

Jules White is married and lives in a suburb of Los Angeles.

Del Lord

Jules White directed his first Stooges short in 1938. However, another frequent Stooges director, Del Lord, began directing the team as early as 1934. "Without Del Lord," says Edward Bernds, yet another Stooges director, "the Three Stooges probably would never have survived as a comedy team." Lord is credited for having helped the Stooges shape their grotesque characterizations into likably dumb personalities.

Lord started out in the movie business working in tandem with Jules White. Lord eventually became a stunt driver for Mack Sennett and soon rose to the ranks of director. Sennett even dubbed Lord "the greatest pie thrower in the

Del Lord, as he appeared while working for Mack Sennett in the mid-1920s. (Photo courtesy of Earl Lord.)

movie business." Strangely enough, Lord never directed any of the Stooges' classic society pie-fight episodes, though Lord's first Stooges film, **Pop Goes the Easel** (1935), does include some pretty substantial clay throwing.

Edward Bernds remembers Lord as a top-notch comedy director and writer, despite the fact that he was somewhat less than bookish. Bernds remembers that when a suggestion was offered in a script Lord would pencil in "mabe" next to it. That meant he would consider it.

Lord, who died in the early 1960s, made a total of 39 short subjects with the Three Stooges.

Ed Bernds

Ed Bernds, another frequent shorts director, also wrote 10 Stooges films. Bernds's friends, in fact, used to call him "one of the biggest writers in Hollywood." Mr. Bernds, you see, is over six feet tall.

Despite the kidding, Bernds's stature as a writer, as well as director, is more than physical. For years he served as head sound man for director Frank Capra. When Bernds decided he wanted to become a director himself, it was Capra who put in a good word for him with Harry Cohn, head of Columbia Pictures. Bernds got his break and eventually rose to the position of feature film director. He directed feature films, including three Three Stooges features, throughout the 1940s, '50s, and '60s.

On and off, Bernds worked with the Stooges longer than any other director, though not always in that position. He was a sound man on their very first starring film appearance and was still working with them more than three decades later as a director on their television series.

Bernds was a sound technician on *Woman Haters* (1934), the Three Stooges' first film as an independent comedy team. A decade later Bernds began directing. In 1945 he wrote and directed what critic Leonard Maltin has called the best short the Three Stooges ever made, *Micro-Phonies* (1945). Altogether Bernds directed 25 Stooge shorts.

Bernds often worked closely with Elwood Ullman, who contributed what are generally regarded as the Stooges' best scripts. In 1952, both Bernds and Ullman left Columbia Pictures to work on the Bowery Boys features at Allied Artists Studios. Together, they virtually created a comedy team from the group. The Bernds-Ullman episodes showcased the patsyish qualities of Bowery Boy Huntz Hall and played up the bossy, bullyish nature of his partner, Leo Gorcey. Through Bernds's direction and Ullman's writing, the pair brought a Stooges-like quality to the Bowery Boys films.

Bernds retired from directing in the 1960s. Bernds (a native of Chicago) and his wife live in the Los Angeles area.

Ed Bernds, at his old desk in Hollywood. (Photo courtesy of Ed Bernds.)

RELATIVELY SPEAKING

Like many other successful film performers, the Three Stooges often brought in their own relatives to work on their motion picture projects.

Moe Howard's son-in-law, Norman Maurer, became extremely influential in the Stooges' career. He produced, directed, and even served as a writer on their feature films. *The Three Stooges Go Around the World in a Daze* (1963) was the first Stooges feature produced *and* directed by Maurer. In addition, Maurer wrote the story, which was developed into a screenplay by Elwood Ullman. Moe's grandson, Jeffrey Maurer, even turned up in the film in a small role.

Larry Fine's son-in-law, Don Lamond, also worked in a handful of Stooges features, as an actor and a narrator. As a narrator, he introduced *The Three Stooges Meet Hercules* and *The Three Stooges in Orbit,* both made in 1962 and both produced by Norman Maurer.

Recently, Maurer and his wife, Joan, announced a number of new Three Stooges–themed projects. A recent issue of *American Film* magazine stated that the Maurers are developing projects ranging from prime-time television specials to a complete Broadway show.

The *Daily Variety* recently reported that Moe Howard's grandsons, Jeffrey and Michael Maurer, are writing a brand-new screenplay involving Three Stooges–like characters. The title? "Dirty Larry, Dirty Moe, and Dirty Curly."

SOLITARY REFINEMENT

Although each of the Third Stooges achieved his greatest

contemporary fame through appearances with the team itself, all of them worked alone at one time or another, honing their comic skills as solo performers.

★   ★   ★

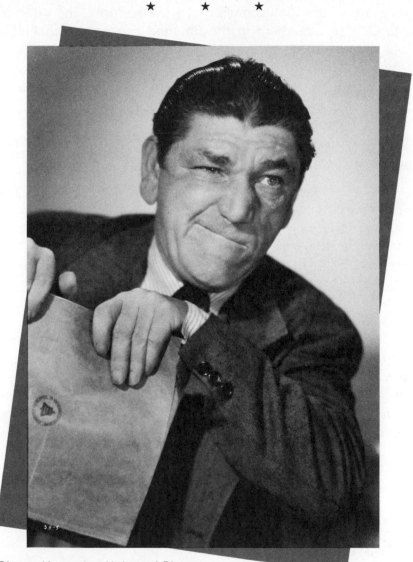

Shemp Howard at Universal Pictures.
(Photo courtesy of Universal Pictures,
copyright 1940.)

The first Third Stooge to go solo was Shemp Howard. He left the group in the early 1930s to pursue a career as a single performer. In *The Bank Dick* (1940), starring W. C. Fields, Shemp frequently ad-libbed routines during the shooting of the film, scenes that were so funny the director intended to use them in the finished product. "But Fields took Shemp aside one day," recalls Shemp's widow, Babe Howard. "He said, 'You know, there is only *one* funnyman in this picture. You understand?' Shemp ignored him, because the director loved it. But none of it ended up in the finished movie, because Fields saw to it that it was all cut out! And Shemp would come home and be terribly frustrated, because his best work would never show up in the movie."

★   ★   ★

Joe Besser, the most prolific "solo Stooge," with photos of many of his fellow performers. (Photo courtesy of Edward McCullough.)

The most prolific of the Third Stooges was Joe Besser. He has made several hundred movies on his own, as well as innumerable radio and TV appearances. He was a regular on Abbott and Costello's television series, "The Abbott and Costello Show," as Stinky, the duo's repulsive little next-door neighbor. He also turned up in their feature film *Africa Screams* (1949). In this one he plays a sissified butler who accompanies the comic duo on a safari. Shemp Howard also appeared in this film, as a nearsighted "sharpshooter."

★　　　★　　　★

The least prolific solo Third Stooge was Curly Howard. He only made a handful of movie appearances without his partners. Teamed at MGM with a pair of comics named George Givot and Joe Callahan, Curly did a couple of short subjects, including one titled *Wax Museum* (1933). Givot and Callahan more or less took the place of Curly's Stooge partners, Moe Howard and Larry Fine, who were working under different contracts at the time.

IN PRAISE OF OLDER STOOGES

Although it's one of the best-kept secrets in Hollywood, the Three Stooges weren't the only comedy ensemble to rise from the ranks of the "Ted Healy Stooges." Over the years a number of other comedy groups bearing the Stooges name surfaced, with varying degrees of success.

★　　　★　　　★

Ted Healy and his Stooges at MGM Studios in the early 1930s. Healy helped launch the careers of more than a dozen different Stoogelike performers. (From the MGM release Dancing Lady *© 1933 Metro-Goldwyn-Mayer Corporation. Copyright renewed 1960 by Metro-Goldwyn-Mayer Inc.)*

The original Ted Healy Stooges ensemble was formed in 1925. This group consisted of three comics named Lou Warren, Dick Hakins, and Shemp Howard. About a year later Warren left the group, never to return to the fold. Hakins also left the group due to illness but returned several years later. During the interim period Hakins developed his skill as—believe it or not—a popular songwriter. He scored some Broadway shows and even sold music while on tour with another comedy act overseas. In England, for example, his song "Saying Goodbye to Love" turned up on the flip side of Cole Porter's "Night and Day." Hakins worked with Healy again in the early 1930s but retired from comedy shortly after Healy's death in 1937.

★　　★　　★

Another "lost" Stooges trio was formed in the early 1930s. After Lou Warren and Dick Hakins left Ted Healy in the 1920s, Shemp Howard brought in his brother Moe and Larry Fine as replacements. But Shemp and his partners also left Healy in the 1930s, and yet another replacement trio was needed. Healy brought back Dick Hakins, along with Hakins's friends Jack Wolf and Mousie Garner, who were cousins. Jack Wolf died in the 1960s; his son, Warner Wolf, is now a sportscaster with CBS television.

★　　★　　★

Yet *another* Stooges trio—this one actually calling itself the "Three Stooges"—turned up in the 1930s. In 1934, Skins Miller, Sid Walker, and Jack Harling appeared in the Universal feature film **Gift of Gab** as the "Three Stooges," despite the fact that they bore no relation to the Columbia Pictures trio. Curiously enough, the Columbia trio also made its first movie appearance as the "Three Stooges" in 1934.

★　　★　　★

The last known trio of Stooges surfaced in Hollywood in 1974. It was called the "New Three Stooges," and consisted of Frank Mitchell (playing "the boss"), Mousie Garner (playing "the middleman"), and Joe DeRita (playing the "patsy").

The "New Three Stooges": Joe DeRita,
Mousie Garner (who was also a Stooge
B.C.—Before Curly), and Frank Mitchell.
(Photo courtesy of Frank Mitchell.)

All three were adept at verbal and visual comedy. Mitchell, in fact, even worked as a Stooges stuntman during their Columbia years. The trio made a handful of personal appearances until Joe DeRita's eyesight began to fail, and the team was forced to break up.

PLAYING IT STRAIGHT

Like most of the major physical comedians of their ilk—Lou Costello, Jerry Lewis, and others—the Three Stooges also relied on straight men for stage appearances.

The function of the straight man has traditionally been to serve as a foundation or backboard for the wild nonsense of the comic. In the Stooges' case, their straight man had three times as much trouble on his hands.

★　　★　　★

The team's original "straight" personality was a tall Irishman named Jack Walsh. He appeared with the trio of Moe Howard, his brother Shemp, and Larry Fine in vaudeville during the early 1930s. Ironically, Walsh also served as straight man for another Stooges trio—Jack Wolf, Dick Hakins, and Mousie Garner—in the mid-1930s. Walsh was much taller than the Stooges, and this served as a nice contrast to their squat appearances.

★　　★　　★

In the late 1930s the Three Stooges—comprised of Moe Howard, his brother Curly, and Larry Fine—often appeared in vaudeville with actor Eddie Laughton as their "straight." Laughton also appeared in films with the Stooges, usually in small supporting roles, throughout the '30s and '40s. Like Walsh, he was taller than the Stooges and often wore dapper clothing to offset the grotesque appearance of the slapstick trio.

*Jack Walsh, the Stooges' first straight man, with
(from left) Dick Hakins, Jack Wolf, and Mousie
Garner in the early 1930s. (Photo courtesy of Dick
Hakins.)*

SUPPORT FROM THE RANKS

During their nearly quarter of a century with Columbia Pictures Short Subjects Department the Three Stooges worked with various supporting actors, many of them talented comic performers in their own right.

Bud Jamison

The first Stooges "regular" was Bud Jamison. Jamison was extremely versatile; he could play everything from a tough western badman to an effeminate servant. And he did them all convincingly. In addition, Jamison was a good dialect performer. In **Whoops I'm an Indian** (1936) he played a burly French fur trapper. In **Termites of 1938** (1938) he was an English lord, complete with handlebar mustache and monocle. And in **Mutts to You** (1938), Jamison turned up in perhaps his most familiar characterization—a friendly Irish cop.

Jamison appeared in the Stooges' first Columbia short, **Woman Haters** (1934). His last was **Crash Goes the Hash,** released 10 years later.

Jamison, a Christian Scientist, died in 1944 when he refused to have an infection treated.

On the following page is a listing of Bud Jamison's appearances in Three Stooges short subjects.

1. *Woman Haters* (1934). As president of club.
2. *Men in Black* (1934). As doctor.
3. *Uncivil Warriors* (1935). As Confederate colonel.
4. *Hoi Polloi* (1935). As butler.
5. *Three Little Beers* (1935). As president of brewery.
6. *Ants in the Pantry* (1936). As pianist.
7. *Movie Maniacs* (1936). As studio boss.
8. *Disorder in the Court* (1936). As defense attorney.
9. *A Pain in the Pullman* (1936). As manager of troupe.
10. *Whoops I'm an Indian* (1936). As fur trapper.
11. *Dizzy Doctors* (1937). As policeman.
12. *Back to the Woods* (1937). As court clerk.
13. *Termites of 1938* (1938). As English lord.
14. *Wee Wee Monsieur* (1938). As Foreign Legion officer.
15. *Healthy, Wealthy and Dumb* (1938). As hotel detective.
16. *Violent Is the Word for Curly* (1938). As service station boss.
17. *Tassels in the Air* (1938). As socialite's husband.
18. *Mutts to You* (1938). As policeman.
19. *Three Little Sew and Sews* (1939). As policeman.
20. *We Want Our Mummy* (1939). As museum curator.
21. *Three Sappy People* (1939). As butler.
22. *A Plumbing We Will Go* (1940). As policeman.
23. *Dutiful But Dumb* (1941). As government official.
24. *All the World's a Stooge* (1941). As policeman.
25. *I'll Never Heil Again* (1941). As government official.
26. *An Ache in Every Stake* (1941). As baker.
27. *Loco Boy Makes Good* (1942). As landlord.
28. *Three Smart Saps* (1942). As party guest.
29. *Even as I.O.U.* (1942). As policeman.
30. *Sock-a-Bye Baby* (1942). As policeman.
31. *Dizzy Detectives* (1943). As police chief.
32. *Back from the Front* (1943). As Nazi sailor.
33. *Three Little Twirps* (1943). As plainclothes policeman.
34. *I Can Hardly Wait* (1943). As dentist.
35. *Phony Express* (1943). As bandit leader.
36. *Crash Goes the Hash* (1944). As butler.

Vernon Dent

Vernon Dent appeared in more Stooges films than any of their other supporting players.

Because of the tiny budgets inherent to short-subject production, Columbia relied heavily on the versatility of its supporting players. Vernon Dent quickly became a mainstay of the studio's shorts division, and turned up in dozens of Stooges films. He worked with the Three Stooges for 19 years.

Dent's first Stooges film was **Half Shot Shooters** (1936). His last actual Stooges movie appearance was in **Knutzy Knights** (1955), though old film featuring Dent turned up in later shorts.

Dent retired from show business and later contracted diabetes. He was a Christian Scientist as well, and he died in the early 1960s after refusing to take insulin.

Below is a listing of Vernon Dent's appearances in Three Stooges short subjects.

1. *Half Shot Shooters* (1936). As restaurant patron.
2. *Slippery Silks* (1936). As owner of antique.
3. *Dizzy Doctors* (1937). As hospital administrator.
4. *Back to the Woods* (1937). As pilgrim leader.
5. *Wee Wee Monsieur* (1938). As sultan.
6. *Tassels in the Air* (1938). As office building manager.
7. *Mutts to You* (1938). As landlord.
8. *Three Little Sew and Sews* (1939). As party guest.
9. *A-Ducking They Did Go* (1939). As vegetarian.
10. *Saved by the Belle* (1939). As revolutionist.
11. *Yes We Have No Bonanza* (1939). As sheriff.
12. *Nutty But Nice* (1940). As doctor.
13. *How High Is Up?* (1940). As construction boss.

14. *From Nurse to Worse* (1940). As doctor.
15. *No Census, No Feeling* (1940). As party guest.
16. *So Long, Mr. Chumps* (1941). As policeman.
17. *Dutiful But Dumb* (1941). As magazine editor.
18. *I'll Never Heil Again* (1941). As government official.
19. *An Ache in Every Stake* (1941). As husband.
20. *In the Sweet Pie and Pie* (1941). As senator.
21. *Three Smart Saps* (1942). As party guest.
22. *Loco Boy Makes Good* (1942). As magician.
23. *Cactus Makes Perfect* (1942). As desperado.
24. *Matri-Phony* (1942). As emperor.
25. *Even as I.O.U.* (1942). As man in car.
26. *They Stooge to Conga* (1943). As Nazi agent.
27. *Back from the Front* (1943). As Nazi sailor.
28. *Higher Than a Kite* (1943). As Nazi official.
29. *Crash Goes the Hash* (1944). As newspaper editor.
30. *Busy Buddies* (1944). As restaurant patron.
31. *Idle Roomers* (1944). As husband.
32. *No Dough, Boys* (1944). As Nazi agent.
33. *Booby Dupes* (1945). As naval officer.
34. *Idiots Deluxe* (1945). As judge.
35. *Beer Barrel Polecats* (1946). As prison warden.
36. *A Bird in the Head* (1946). As mad scientist.
37. *Three Little Pirates* (1946). As governor.
38. *Half-Wits Holiday* (1947). As professor.
39. *Out West* (1947). As doctor.
40. *Sing a Song of Six Pants* (1947). As police detective.
41. *Shivering Sherlocks* (1948). As police detective.
42. *Squareheads of the Round Table* (1948). As king.
43. *Heavenly Daze* (1948). As attorney.
44. *Mummy's Dummies* (1948). As pharoah.
45. *Fiddlers Three* (1948). As king.
46. *Hokus Pokus* (1949). As claims adjustor.
47. *Fuelin' Around* (1949). As government official.
48. *Malice in the Palace* (1949). As restaurant patron.
49. *Punchy Cowpunchers* (1950). As cavalry colonel.
50. *Studio Stoops* (1950). As police captain.

51. *Three Arabian Nuts* (1951). As collector.
52. *Scrambled Brains* (1951). As father.
53. *The Tooth Will Out* (1951). As dean of school.
54. *Pest Man Wins* (1951). As party guest.
55. *A Missed Fortune* (1952). As hotel manager.
56. *Listen, Judge* (1952). As judge.
57. *Booty and the Beast* (1953). As policeman.
58. *Rip, Sew and Stitch* (1953). As police detective.*
59. *Income Tax Sappy* (1954). As IRS official.
60. *Pals and Gals* (1954). As doctor.*
61. *Musty Musketeers* (1954). As king.
62. *Knutzy Knights* (1954). As king.
63. *Of Cash and Hash* (1955). As police captain.*
64. *Bedlam in Paradise* (1955). As attorney.*
65. *Flagpole Jitters* (1956). As claims adjustor.*
66. *Rumpus in the Harem* (1956). As restaurant patron.*
67. *Hot Stuff* (1956). As government official.*
68. *Guns a Poppin'* (1957). As judge.*

Emil Sitka

The only supporting player inducted as an actual *member* of the Three Stooges was Emil Sitka. In the handful of Stooges shorts in which he appeared, more often than not he stole the show from the starring performers. Moe Howard enjoyed his work so much that he asked him to join the Stooges after Larry Fine retired in the 1970s.

---

*Old footage only.

Virtually every one of Sitka's film characterizations was a standout. He specialized in playing elderly characters, despite the fact that he was a fairly young man at the time. One of Sitka's funniest performances was in **Gents in a Jam** (1952). Playing the role of "Uncle Phineas," he spent most of his screen time receiving various kinds of physical abuse. Sitka may very well have set a record for martyrdom among supporting players. In this episode alone he is: (1) knocked flat onto his face by a swinging door, (2) rendered unconscious when a vase is broken over his head, and (3) kicked in the chin by a woman running at full speed!

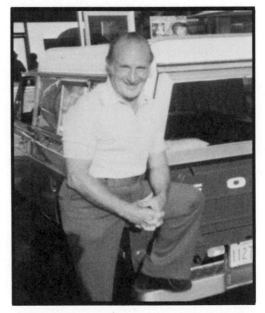

Emil Sitka, the Stooges'
versatile supporting player,
out of character (opposite
page), in character (above),
and as he looks today
(right). (Photos on opposite
page and above courtesy of
Emil Sitka; photo at right
courtesy of Edward
McCullough.)

Sitka's first Three Stooges short was Curly Howard's last, **Half-Wits Holiday** (1947). His last short was **Flying Saucer Daffy** (1958). In addition, Sitka appeared in all of the Stooges' Columbia feature films in the 1960s. In 1975 Sitka was set to replace Larry Fine and appear with Moe Howard and Joe DeRita in a feature film to be produced by independent entrepreneur Sam Sherman. The appearance was canceled, however, when it was learned that Moe was suffering from cancer.

Sitka is widowed and resides in Camarillo, California.

Below is a listing of Emil Sitka's appearances in Three Stooges short subjects.

1. *Half-Wits Holiday* (1947). As butler.
2. *Hold That Lion* (1947). As attorney.
3. *Brideless Groom* (1947). As justice of the peace.
4. *All Gummed Up* (1947). As landlord.
5. *Pardon My Clutch* (1948). As lunatic.
6. *Who Done It?* (1949). As wealthy uncle.
7. *Fuelin' Around* (1949). As professor.
8. *Vagabond Loafers* (1949). As party host.
9. *Punchy Cowpunchers* (1950). As army captain.
10. *Hugs and Mugs* (1950). As storage clerk.
11. *Three Hams on Rye* (1950). As theatrical producer.
12. *Slaphappy Sleuths* (1950). As service station customer.
13. *Scrambled Brains* (1951). As doctor.
14. *Merry Mavericks* (1951). As jailer.
15. *The Tooth Will Out* (1951). As cook.
16. *Hula-La-La* (1951). As studio boss.
17. *Pest Man Wins* (1951). As butler.
18. *Listen, Judge* (1952). As cook.
19. *Gents in a Jam* (1952). As wealthy uncle.
20. *Loose Loot* (1953). As attorney.*
21. *Bubble Trouble* (1953). As landlord.
22. *Shot in the Frontier* (1954). As justice of the peace.
23. *Gypped in the Penthouse* (1955). As member of club.

24. *Stone Age Romeos* (1955). As museum curator.
25. *Husbands Beware* (1955). As justice of the peace.
26. *For Crimin' Out Loud* (1955). As councilman.
27. *Hot Stuff* (1956). As professor.*
28. *Scheming Schemers* (1956). As party host.
29. *Commotion on the Ocean* (1956). As reporter.
30. *Space Ship Sappy* (1957). As master of ceremonies.
31. *Horsing Around* (1957). As circus worker.
32. *Outer Space Jitters* (1958). As professor.
33. *Quiz Whiz* (1958). As IRS official.
34. *Pies and Guys* (1958). As butler.
35. *Flying Saucer Daffy* (1958). As police detective.

LEGITIMATE STOOGE DEBUT

Many actors and actresses started out doing bit or supporting parts in the Columbia Three Stooges short subjects. Listed below are some of the now-famous performers who worked with the Stooges in the 1930s, '40s, and '50s.

★   ★   ★

Walter Brennan played a train conductor in *Woman Haters* (1934), the Stooges' first Columbia comedy. The Oscar-winning Brennan had trouble remembering his lines.

★   ★   ★

Lucille Ball appeared as a gangster's moll in *Three Little Pigskins* (1934)—complete with blonde hair.

★   ★   ★

---

*Old footage only.

These three times two? Now that's frightening.
(© 1933 Metro-Goldwyn-Mayer Corporation.
Copyright renewed 1960 by Metro-Goldwyn-Mayer
Inc.)

Lloyd Bridges had one line—as a telephone caller—in *They Stooge to Conga* (1943).

★　★　★

Jock Mahoney—originally billed as "Jacques O'Mahoney"—made a number of appearances with the Stooges. His first film with the Stooges was *Out West* (1947), in which he played a cowboy "hero" who kept missing out on the action.

★　★　★

And **Dan Blocker**—best known as "Hoss" from NBC's "Bonanza" series—turned up as a hideous zombie in *Outer Space Jitters* (1957).

TRIPLE DUPLICATES

Throughout their movie career the Three Stooges used a number of doubles and stuntmen to take on some of their more dangerous physical gags.

★　★　★

Moe's double was Johnny Kascier, who occasionally turned up in speaking roles as well. For example, Kascier played the part of the bellhop in *Brideless Groom* (1947). Larry's double was Teddy Mangean, while Frank Mitchell and Hurley Breen both doubled for Shemp. In addition to doubling for Moe, Johnny Kascier occasionally doubled for Curly.

★　★　★

Sometimes even the Stooges' stand-ins wound up getting hurt. The worst accident occurred during the shooting of *Three Little Pigskins* (1934), starring Curly Howard. A comic football game highlighted this episode, featuring the Loyola University football team. The college players tackled the Stooges' doubles, along with some other supporting actors in the scene. As a result, everyone but the Curly "fake" wound up with broken bones. Curly's double was protected from injury because he was wearing heavy padding.

★　　　★　　　★

By the time Shemp Howard rejoined the Stooges in the late 1940s he was already more than 50 years old. Accordingly, he could hardly be expected to take some of the flips and falls that were occasionally required of his character. In *Who Done It?* (1949), for example, a stuntman was on hand for a very strenuous slapstick sequence. In this scene Shemp supposedly swallows a poison drink and goes into a wild seizure of flips, falls, and somersaults. The stuntman performed most of the acrobatic stuff, while shots of Shemp choking, gasping, and slapping his neck were later edited in. What resulted was a hilarious bit of physical comedy that looks as if Shemp himself is doing most of the slapstick.

★　　　★　　　★

Shemp's double was really put to work in a handful of "Shemp" shorts released in the 1950s. These were all produced after Shemp Howard died in 1955, yet the films continued to use the "Shemp" character as the "Third Stooge." Joe Palma, a frequent Stooges supporting player, played the role of the Shemp "fake," seen briefly and only from behind. Only four episodes were made using the phony Shemp: *Rumpus in the Harem, Hot Stuff, Scheming Schemers,* and *Commotion on the Ocean.*

★   ★   ★

The greatest number of Stooges fakes were used in *A Merry Mix Up.* In this one a *half-dozen* doubles were required! The Stooges play themselves, as well as two sets of lookalike brothers. Altogether, through use of editing, split-screen photography, and a lot of stand-ins, nine Stooges—Moe Howard, Larry Fine, and Joe Besser in triplicate—appeared in the film.

Do-It-Yourself Stooge

The Stooges didn't always use doubles—but they weren't always anxious to do the stunts themselves. In *Three Little Sew and Sews* (1939), the closing gag of the film has the Stooges playing angels. To accomplish this effect, the Stooges were hung from piano wire in front of a large process screen. Since Larry was the lightest of the three, he was to be raised to the highest position, with Moe and Curly below him. Larry started complaining, saying that if he fell he could be seriously hurt. So director Del Lord assured him that he could be the low man. Larry agreed to this concession, but as soon as he was strung up Lord gave the prop man the signal to raise Larry to the highest position! "Larry was screaming and yelling," says Ed Bernds, "but Del told him, 'You're up there, and you're gonna *stay* up there until we finish the goddam shot!'" Needless to say, Larry stopped whining and Lord finished the shot.

THE SINCEREST FORM
OF BATTERY

In recent years a number of Three Stooges "impersonators" have popped up on various television variety shows. The first TV series to feature a recurring segment with Three Stooges–like characters was NBC's "Rich Little Show." Norman Maurer Productions, which claims to own the right to license the names and likenesses of the Three Stooges, objected to the usage. According to Norman Maurer, his company reached ". . . a favorable out-of-court settlement with NBC for their unauthorized use of the likenesses of the Three Stooges on the 'Rich Little Show.' "

The most recent semi-regular Stooges impersonators turned up on ABC's "Fridays." The sketches dealt with such "contemporary" topics as punk rock and drug usage. The classic Stooges short subject *Micro-Phonies* served as the basis for one sketch, in which the "Fridays" Stooges, with their bizarre haircuts and behavior, are mistaken for a trio of punk rockers. John Roarke, a "Fridays" regular, played the "Curly" role.

Again, Norman Maurer Productions objected to the use of the Three Stooges characters. The company's attorneys requested that ABC "arrange for the payment of a suitable license fee" for what they termed "unauthorized use and misappropriation of the names and likenesses of the Three Stooges."

★   ★   ★

In addition to these network programs, "Second City Television," the original syndicated series, also featured a sketch involving Three Stooges–type characters. Assuming what was basically the Curly Howard role was John Candy. Candy also paid homage to the comedian in **Stripes** (1981), a Columbia Pictures "army" comedy. Candy played the role of Dewey Oxberger, or "Ox," who happened to look a lot like "Curly" after getting his hair sheared for boot camp.

THE STOOGEPHILE
TRIVIA
BOOK
JEFFREY FORRESTER

2
THE ART OF
ARTLESSNESS

CRUDE FOR THOUGHT

Critic Leonard Maltin once wrote of the Three Stooges, "Their artlessness is in fact their particular 'art.'"

The essence of Stooges comedy has never been evaluated more accurately. Even today, however, the critics are still very much divided when it comes to discussing the comedic contributions of the Three Stooges.

If there's one thing that even the critics will agree on, it's that the Three Stooges cornered the market on sheer crudeness. Some examples are recounted on the following page.

PORTLY WOMAN (to a FRIEND): I think I'd look stunning in that riding habit!

CURLY (to MOE and LARRY): I think I'd have trouble figuring out which one is the horse.

(From *Slippery Silks,* a Columbia short subject of 1936.)

★　　★　　★

MOE (to SOCIETY MATRON): How old are you?

MATRON: How old do I look?

MOE: Oh, you look like a million!

LARRY: Naah, she can't be *that* old.

(From *No Census, No Feeling,* a Columbia short subject of 1940.)

★　　★　　★

COLLEGE MATRON (to MOE): We have a lovely student body!

MOE: Yours wouldn't be too bad, either, if you took off about 20 pounds.

(From *Violent is the Word for Curly,* a Columbia short subject of 1938.)

SLAP SHTICK

Like most other comedians of their ilk, the Three Stooges developed their own distinctive bits of business, known collectively as "shtick." The Stooges accompanied their standard face-slapping and violence routines with a number of clever nonviolent bits, some of which are listed below.

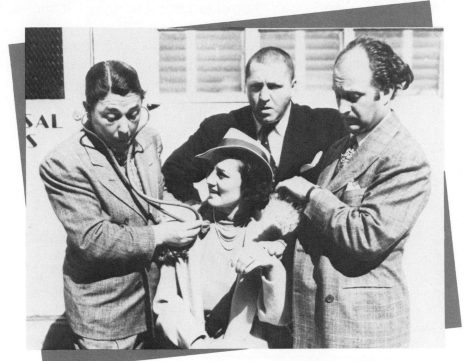

The boys are up to their old shticks again, this time dragging Curly's wife Elaine into the action. (Photo courtesy of Elaine Diamond.)

"Woo-Woo-Woo"

This, of course, is the most frequently imitated aspect of Curly's vocal repertoire. Curly would scream, "woo-woo-woo," whenever he was delighted, frightened, or nervous. It popped up most frequently when the Stooges were on the run from an authority figure. Since Curly Howard patterned his character after comedian Hugh Herbert, there is more than reasonable assumption that he adapted "woo-woo-

woo" from Herbert's own "hoo-hoo-hoo." Strange as it may sound, Herbert actually ended up doing "woo-woo-woo" himself! According to Leonard Maltin, in his book *The Great Movie Shorts,* Herbert's vocal gag was imitated so frequently that "the copy eventually overtook the original."

The Shoulder Spin

The shoulder spin routine was often used by Curly and later by Shemp. Curly would throw himself on the floor, then run around in a circle—laying down—while pivoting on his shoulder. The bit actually originated on the set. It seems Curly couldn't remember his lines, so he simply threw himself onto the floor and started running around in circles.

The Lip Quiver

Just as Curly had his own repertoire of bits and mannerisms that defined his personality, so did Shemp. Shemp developed a bit that can only be described as a lip quiver, which was the logical equivalent to Curly's "woo-woo-woo." The effect can be simulated by sucking in air while emitting a loud, high-pitched sound. Shemp used the quiver, depending on the situation, to express feelings of happiness, fear, or anxiety. He even made the noise while laughing, crying, and snoring.

Curly brings new meaning to the term "mug shot." Facial expressions were, of course, a major facet of Curly's comedy. (Photos courtesy of Jane Howard Hanky.)

The Fighter's Dance

While Curly developed a wide assortment of marches, backsteps, and so forth, Shemp had his own brand of funny footwork. One of the funniest was something that resembled a parody of a fighter's dance. He always managed to work in the gag when his character was required to slug somebody, usually much taller and broader than he was.

Our three cornblowers. (From the MGM release
Hello Pop © 1933 Metro-Goldwyn-Mayer Corporation.
Copyright renewed 1960 by Metro-Goldwyn-
Mayer Inc.)

Shemp's fists would fly past his "victim's" head while he pantomimed skipping rope, danced around like a prizefighter on speed, and made taunting remarks like, "Little too quick for you, eh?" He usually ended up receiving the first punch. Shemp actually *was* an amateur boxer while in the army during the First World War, which is where he acquired much of his facial "character."

COME BLOW YOUR CORN

Intentionally corny jokes were often included in the Stooges films as setups for Moe to launch some sort of physical attack on one of his partners. Below are some examples.

MOE (to CURLY): What's the name of that song?
CURLY: "Don't Chop the Wood, Mother—Father's Coming
    Home with a Load."
      (Curly then receives the standard facial slap.)
(From **Booby Dupes,** a Columbia short subject of 1945.)

★   ★   ★

MOE (to CURLY): Why can't a chicken lay a loaf of bread?
CURLY: 'Cause she ain't got the crust!
    *(Curly then gets smashed on the head with a
    wrench.)*
(From **They Stooge to Conga,** a Columbia short subject of 1943.)

★   ★   ★

CURLY (to MOE): Wait a minute! I've got somethin' to *do* before I die!

　　(Curly pulls out a cream pie and starts eating it.)
MOE: What's the idea of eatin' pie?
CURLY: So I can di-gest right!

　　(Curly then receives a punch in the stomach and is dragged away by his ear.)

(From **Rhythm and Weep,** a Columbia short subject of 1946.)

NURTURING NEW NATURES

The most popular Stooges story premise was the "heredity/environment" controversy—it was the basis for three different Stooges episodes.

These films were **Hoi Polloi** (1935), **Half-Wits Holiday** (1947), and **Pies and Guys** (1958). Curly Howard starred in the first two episodes, and Joe Besser played his role in the last. **Half-Wits Holiday** was basically a reworking of **Hoi Polloi. Pies and Guys,** on the other hand, was a straightforward remake of **Half-Wits Holiday.**

The plot line of all three films has a wealthy professor trying to make gentlemen of the Stooges. In the first version Harry Holmes played the prof; in the second, Vernon Dent; and in the third, Milton Frome.

Each of the films ends in a wild slapstick melee. In the first the Stooges incite a massive riot of physical battery; all the other performers end up slapping, poking, and belting each other in typical Three Stooges style. In the second and final versions the Stooges start massive pie fights. The pie-throwing footage from **Half-Wits Holiday** was lifted almost intact for **Pies and Guys,** with Joe Besser sitting in for Curly Howard.

Gentlemen? *At least they're trying. (From the MGM release* Dancing Lady *© 1933 Metro-Goldwyn-Mayer Corporation. Copyright renewed 1960 by Metro-Goldwyn-Mayer Inc.)*

Moe's wife, Helen Howard, concocted the original story for **Hoi Polloi,** then sold it to Columbia Pictures. Felix Adler, a Columbia staff writer, then wrote the screenplay.

BACK TO THE INSULT MINES

Whenever Moe wished to express verbal, rather than physical, anger at either one of his partners, he simply harked back to his amazing reservoir of uncomplimentary monikers and chose one suitable for the occasion:

applehead

birdbrain

cabbagehead

chiseler

chowderhead

chucklehead

chump

dimwit

dope

doughhead

dumbbell

dunce

fathead

flathead

featherbrain

halfwit

idiot

ignoramus

imbecile

knucklehead

lunkhead

mongoose

moron

muttonhead

nitwit

numbskull

porcupine

possumpuss

puddinhead

sap

sawdusthead

skillethead

spongehead

stupe

weasel

worm

And, lest we forget, *stooge.*

THE TAMING OF THE STOOGE

A popular comedy premise often used by the Three Stooges was that of poking fun at various phobias. The Third Stooge was usually the one with the screw loose, and many of the team's funniest films were built on this idea.

Equally funny were the ridiculous "cures" or "tranquilizers" for these phobias. Listed below are some of the classics:

Tuneophobia

In their 1934 film **Punch Drunks** Curly slugs everyone within reach whenever he hears the song "Pop Goes the Weasel." The Stooges actually use Curly's malady to advantage by making a prizefighter out of him. Moe serves as trainer, and Larry provides the rousing music that drives Curly nuts.

Cure: Stop the music.

Rodentophobia

In the Stooges' 1935 short **Horses Collars** Curly goes out of his mind whenever he sees mice—"because his father was a rat." This comes in handy when the boys tangle with a gang of western badmen. Curly winds up beating up just about everybody in the joint until his partners stop him.

Cure: Feed him cheese.

The Stooges in their first screen riot scene, from
Beer and Pretzels (1933), starring Ted Healy. It
would be three more years before the Stooges
threw their first movie pie.

*(© 1933 Metro-Goldwyn-Mayer Corporation.
Copyright renewed 1960 by Metro-Goldwyn-
Mayer Inc.)*

THE ART OF ARTLESSNESS   61

Scentophobia

The team's 1937 episode **Grips, Grunts and Groans** features a subplot in which Curly goes wild whenever he smells Wild Hyacinth perfume. This allows him to masquerade as a wrestler, and he winds up knocking out his opponent—as well as practically everybody else in the place.
Cure: Tickle his foot.

A PIE FOR A PIE

Although virtually every slapstick comedian from Hollywood's golden era tossed a pie or two during his career, the Three Stooges probably threw more pastry and prompted more slapstick "retaliation" than any other comedians of the sound era.

During their tenure at Columbia Pictures hundreds of pies were thrown in the name of comedy. Most of these were thrown by Moe Howard, who was renowned for his pastry-flinging abilities. Sometimes more than 100 pies were thrown for a sequence that might last only a few minutes.

★　　★　　★

The first full-fledged pie fight to turn up in a Stooges movie was in the short subject **Slippery Silks** (1936). In this one the boys inherit their uncle's gown shop and become instant fashion designers. On hand at a special fashion show is, of course, a table full of pastry. It isn't long before the Stooges begin tossing the stuff, most of which finds its way to the powdered faces of the society women attending the show.

★　　★　　★

Probably the wildest pie fight of all turned up in **Pest Man Wins** (1951), with Shemp Howard as one of the Stooges. In addition to new footage shot specifically for this film, clips from two different Stooges pie-fight episodes, **In the Sweet Pie and Pie** (1941) and **Half-Wits Holiday** (1947), were spliced in. Use of stock footage made it look as if a huge cast had been assembled for the low-budget short subject!

★　　★　　★

The last pie fight short the Stooges did was **Pies and Guys** (1958). This film also includes footage from **Half-Wits Holiday** (1947); in fact, the pie-throwing sequence from the original is used almost intact, with only minimal editing.

★　　★　　★

The Stooges produced eight short subjects that ended with at least one or two pies being thrown in a "polite society" setting. Five featured Curly, two were with Shemp, and **Pies and Guys** was the only pie fight episode featuring Joe Besser.

SOMETIMES IT HURTS TO ASK

Strange as it may sound, the Stooges often *asked* for punishment:

Setup: *Moe thinks Curly has just tossed a huge radio at his head.*

MOE (to CURLY): Tell me—do you like the radio?
CURLY: Certainly! I *love* it!
MOE: You got it.

Result: *Curly gets the radio smashed over his head like a straw hat.*

(From **Idle Roomers,** a Columbia short subject of 1944.)

★　　★　　★

Setup: *Shemp has accidentally stabbed Moe in the posterior with a spiked instrument.*

MOE (to SHEMP): What would you rather have—a shoeful of dollar bills or two socks of five?
SHEMP: I'll take the two socks!
MOE: You got 'em.

Result: *Moe slams both of his fists into Shemp's unprotected eyes.*

(From **Hot Scots,** a Columbia short subject of 1948.)

★　　★　　★

And this classic retaliation, where Moe lets his "victim" have it simply for making a silly remark:

Setup: *Curly is holding an unwrapped, unsmoked cigar to his ear.*

MOE (to CURLY): What are you doin'?
CURLY: Listenin' to the band!
MOE: Would you like to hear some birdies?
CURLY: I'd love it!
MOE: Take off your hat.

Result: *Moe smacks Curly's head so hard that he hears what sound like chirping birds.*

(From **Crash Goes the Hash,** a Columbia short subject of 1944.)

NOBLE TITLES

As Leonard Maltin pointed out in *Movie Comedy Teams,* "Often the titles of the Stooges films were better than the films themselves."

Many of the Three Stooges short subjects used titles that were parodies of other movie titles, literary works, popular songs, or, most frequently, famous expressions:

Movie Parodies

Men in Black (1934) .... *Men in White* (1934)
Three Little Pigskins (1934) .... *Three Little Pigs* (1933)
Violent is the Word for Curly (1938) .... *Valiant Is the Word for Carrie* (1934)
Nutty But Nice (1940) .... *Naughty But Nice* (1939)
Boobs in Arms (1940) .... *Babes in Arms* (1939)
So Long, Mr. Chumps (1941) .... *Goodbye, Mr. Chips* (1939)

Literary Parodies

All the World's a Stooge (1941) .... "All the World's a Stage"
They Stooge to Conga (1943) .... "She Stoops to Conquer"
Vagabond Loafers (1949) .... "Vagabond Lovers"
Three Arabian Nuts (1951) .... "Arabian Nights"
Booty and the Beast (1953) .... "Beauty and the Beast"
Oil's Well That Ends Well (1958) .... "All's Well that Ends Well"

Song Parodies

Pop Goes the Easel (1935) .... "Pop Goes the Weasel"
Yes We Have No Bonanza (1939) .... "Yes We Have No Bananas"
Three Sappy People (1939)............... "Three Sleepy People"
A Plumbing We Will Go (1940) .... "A-Hunting We Will Go"
I'll Never Heil Again (1941) .... "I'll Never Smile Again"
In the Sweet Pie and Pie (1941) .... "In the Sweet By and By"
Sock-a-Bye Baby (1942) .... "Rock-a-Bye Baby"
Beer Barrel Polecats (1946) .... "Beer Barrel Polka"
Sing a Song of Six Pants (1947) ...... "Sing a Song of Sixpence"
Muscle Up a Little Closer (1957)..... "Cuddle Up a Little Closer"

Expression Parodies

Pardon My Scotch (1935) .... "Pardon my French."
Ants in the Pantry (1936).................... "ants in the pants"
Grips, Grunts and Groans (1937) ... "gripes, grunts, and groans"
Healthy, Wealthy and Dumb (1938) .... "healthy, wealthy,
and wise"
Mutts to You (1938) .... "nuts to you"
Saved by the Belle (1939) .... "saved by the bell"
Oily to Bed, Oily to Rise (1939)....... "early to bed, early to rise"
From Nurse to Worse (1940)................ "from bad to worse"
Dutiful But Dumb (1941) .... "beautiful but dumb"
Loco Boy Makes Good (1942) .... "Local boy makes good."
Cactus Makes Perfect (1942) .... "Practice makes perfect."
The Yoke's on Me (1944) .... "The joke's on me."
A Bird in the Head (1945) .... "a bird in the hand"
Rhythm and Weep (1946) .... "Read 'em and weep."
Hold That Lion (1947)......................... "Hold that line."
Crime on Their Hands (1948).............. "time on their hands"
Love at First Bite (1950).................... "love at first sight"
A Snitch in Time (1951) .... "a stitch in time"

The Tooth Will Out (1951) . . . . "The truth will out."
Pest Man Wins (1951) . . . . "The best man wins."
For Crimin' Out Loud (1956) . . . . "for cryin' out loud"

SHEARED INSANITY

The Stooges' goofy haircut concept was devised by Ted Healy, who felt that each of his Stooges should have some kind of distinguishing physical trademark. The haircuts, used by the Stooges almost consistently throughout their careers, did the trick.

★   ★   ★

Moe Howard wore his naturally dark hair in bangs, which gave him a beetle-browed appearance. Moe himself described it as a "bedpan" haircut. Sometimes his hair was used for more than just subliminal comic effect; in many Stooges comedies a rush of air was blown up under Moe's bangs, causing them literally to stand on end! This usually indicated terror and brought new meaning to the term "hair-raising fear."

★   ★   ★

Larry Fine allowed his naturally frizzy hair to bush around his scalp, making a neat crown across the top of his head. Its length and consistency were perfect for pulling, yanking, and tearing, at least from a Stooge's point of view. Larry's hair was also used as an actual prop in many of the Stooges' routines.

In one episode, the classic **Tassels in the Air** (1938), Curly is suffering from an aversion to tassels—he goes crazy whenever he sees one, and the only way to calm him is to tickle his chin. When Curly goes wild at a society bridge

The Stooges' hairstyles were the most important aspect of their physical appearances. (Photo courtesy of Stephen Cox and Joyce Bishoff.)

party Moe soothes him by ripping a handful of hair from Larry's head and rubbing it under Curly's chin. When Curly relaxes Moe hands the wad of hair back to Larry.

"My hair!" protests Larry.

"What are you complainin' about?" snaps Moe. "I gave it *back* to you, didn't I?"

This bit was actually accomplished by embedding a handful of synthetic wig hair into Larry's own bush of frizz, which Moe would then yank out—accompanied by a ripping sound effect.

★   ★   ★

While each of the Third Stooges had his own distinctive haircut, none was as distinctive as Curly Howard's. Curly decided on his haircut after Ted Healy complained that his own hair—beautiful, wavy, and brown—just wasn't funny enough. Curly's brother Shemp, who preceded him in the Healy Stooges ensemble, talked Curly into shaving it all off—but Curly demanded the nickname in return. The simple hairstyle perfectly complemented his simpleton personality.

THE SOUND OF MAYHEM

The Three Stooges' movie mayhem was almost always embellished with sound effects, geared to make the violence audible as well as visual. Here are some examples of the different sound effects used to increase the dramatic content of the Stooges' physical abuse.

Facial Slaps

A simple slapstick was used for this effect. However, when a character was required to really "wind up" and belt the Stooges, often a windlike sound effect was added prior to the slapping sound.

Stomach Punches

A kettledrum was often used to accomplish the sound of this belly banger, which turned up in virtually every film the Stooges made.

Eye Pokes

A violin or ukulele pluck actually made this bit appear to be *less* painful. In the Stooges' early films sound did not accompany this gag, except for a grunt of pain from the poor soul on the receiving end. Later, when the sound effects department contributed the sharp plunk, the gag became more obviously farcical.

Hair Ripping

A cloth was torn to accomplish the ripping sound for this bit.

Ear Twists

A ratchet provided the twisting sound necessary for this traditional assault. Ratchets were also used to embellish the twisting of arms, legs, and so forth.

Sometimes the Stooges provided their own sound effects. (From the MGM release Beer and Pretzels © 1933 Metro-Goldwyn-Mayer Corporation. Copyright renewed 1960 by Metro-Goldwyn-Mayer Inc.)

TURNING THE OTHER CHEEK

Physical mayhem was the cornerstone of Three Stooges comedy. The most significant aspect of that mayhem, of course, was the team's obsession with face slapping.

The Three Stooges never made a film without at least a little facial battery. This tradition was started in vaudeville by Ted Healy, the first vaudeville comedian who actually belted his second bananas.

When the Stooges left Healy's act in the early 1930s Moe Howard more or less assumed Healy's role as the leader of the group. As part of his dictatorial responsibilities, it was Moe's duty to keep the other Stooges in line. This was usually best accomplished by dishing out the standard palm-slap to one or both of his partners.

One would think that years of physical battery would tend to wear down the unfortunate Stooges on the receiving end. Moe Howard, however, developed a technique of whacking his partners without really harming them. Director Edward Bernds explains that Moe had a method of slapping with his palm in a way that did not inflict pain. Moe would keep his fingers loose, and this way the slap would be audible and resounding but not nearly as painful as it looked.

The most important aspect of the Stooge slap, of course, was the follow-through. In other words, it was up to the Stooge on the receiving end to make the slap work, either by yelping or twisting his head about as if in pain.

Of course, there were variations on the standard cheek slap. Some of the more popular methods of facial assault are listed below.

Double Cheek Slap

This was accomplished by cracking both cheeks with both hands simultaneously. Sound effects complemented this, of course, with the sound of two slaps at once.

Backhand Slap

This slap was used sparingly, usually only when Moe's physical distance (standing too close to build up any momentum) from his partner prevented him from cracking him with his palm. This slap might have inflicted more comic *pain,* though, considering that Moe's knuckles came into play.

Forehead Slap

Larry's receding hairline was usually on the receiving end of this bit. Moe would reach up and "affectionately" pat him on the dome, then, after Larry's guard was down, whack him full force.

LONG-RUNNING HITS

Here are some of the more frequently used physical abuse techniques the Three Stooges employed in their stage, screen, and television appearances.

The Poke in the Eyes

This famous bit was invented—although quite accidentally—by Shemp Howard. During a card game backstage in the 1930s Shemp accused fellow Stooge Larry Fine of cheating. When Larry denied it Shemp stood up and stuck two fingers into Larry's eyes! Moe Howard, who was always in search of new bits for the act, had found one—although from that point on they never really jabbed each other directly in the eyes. The Stooges eventually abandoned this bit in the 1960s when parental groups complained it was too violent.

"Moe was dynamite with the poke in the eyes," said Larry Fine in the 1970s. "He came very close, but he never hurt anybody. He had a beautiful touch—he could have been a pickpocket!"

The Triple Slap

This gag was concocted by Ted Healy. It was accomplished by slapping one's hand across three faces at once, in a brisk, nonstop motion. After the Stooges went out on their own in the 1930s they often reworked the bit as a double slap—with Moe taking Healy's place as the slapper.

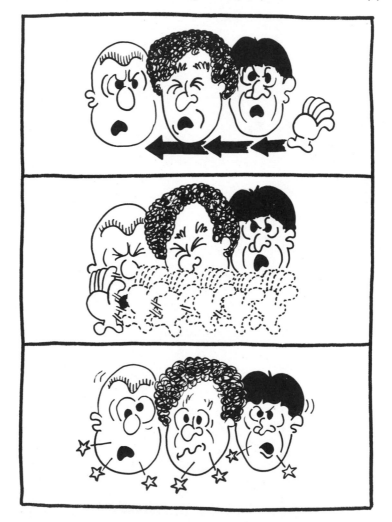

The Nose Tweak

This bit was accomplished by tweaking the bottom of someone's nose with one's index finger. Moe Howard, of course, was usually behind the tweaking. In nonsensical Stooge fashion, this obviously painless tweak frequently generated more mock-pain than the eye poke.

The Chain-Reaction Punch

   This gag required an elaborate setup in order to work properly. Moe would tell one of his partners to relax. Then he'd instruct him to rest a bit, placing his chin on his fist,

and his elbow on his kneecap. Then, after Moe saw to it that his victim's chin was resting securely on his fist, his elbow was on his knee, and his foot was raised far enough off the ground, Moe would violently kick the bottom of his victim's foot. This, of course, would cause a chain reaction, resulting in the victim slugging himself with his own fist.

The Hand-to-Hand Head Clunk

This turned out to be one of the Stooges' most familiar gestures. Moe would hold his fist out in front of him and ask, "See that?" Invariably, one of his partners would reply, "Yeah," and insolently slap Moe's hand. Moe's fist would

swing in a circular motion above his head, landing on the head of the victim. If one of his partners, usually the patsy figure, decided to try the same bit on Moe, the patsy would end up clunking himself on the head. And, as a rule of thumb, the patsy could never quite figure out what had happened, except that his head now hurt twice as much as before.

THE STOOGEPHILE
TRIVIA
BOOK
JEFFREY FORRESTER

3
A LEGACY OF LAUGHTER

FEATURED PERFORMERS

During their lengthy performing career the Three Stooges, with various changes in personnel, appeared in a number of theatrically released feature films. The feature films, in contrast to their 18-minute short subjects, were about an hour or more in length apiece.

★　　★　　★

The Stooges' first feature film appearance was in **Soup to Nuts** (1930), produced at Fox Studios in Hollywood. Ted Healy was the main attraction in this film, with the

Stooges—including Moe Howard, his brother Shemp, and Larry Fine—appearing as supporting players. The Stooges' role was so small that they did not even receive billing in the film's credits. *Soup to Nuts* was also the *only* film in which *four* Stooges appeared: Fred Sanborn, who had worked temporarily with Ted Healy in vaudeville, played the role of the fourth man. None of the Stooges wore gag haircuts in this one.

★   ★   ★

The first cameo appearance the Stooges made in a feature film was in *My Sister Eileen* (1942), starring Rosalind Russell and Brian Aherne. The boys are working beneath Russell's apartment, and at the very end of the film they come popping up from under the floor. This cameo served as the closing gag of the film.

★   ★   ★

The first feature film in which the Stooges received top billing was *Rockin' in the Rockies* (1945), with Curly Howard as Third Stooge. Like their first starring short subject, *Woman Haters* (1934), this one introduces the Stooges as separate characters. Moe is a gold prospector, "Shorty," while Curly and Larry play a couple of vagrants who meet Shorty at a casino. Strangely enough, there is very little slapping, poking, or bopping in this film, probably because Moe is playing a basically "normal" character. This becomes obvious in his initial encounter with Curly and Larry. For the first time in more than a decade, Moe wears his hair combed straight back, temporarily abandoning his traditional cereal-bowl haircut.

★   ★   ★

Curly Howard with Joan Crawford and Ted Healy on the set of Dancing
Lady *(1933), Curly's third feature film appearance with the Stooges.
(© 1933 Metro-Goldwyn-Mayer Corporation. Copyright renewed 1960 by
Metro-Goldwyn-Mayer Inc.)*

The briefest feature film appearance the Stooges ever made was in Stanley Kramer's *It's a Mad Mad Mad Mad World* (1963). In this mammoth comedy extravaganza—featuring a virtual who's who of comedy stars—the Stooges appear on screen for only a few seconds, standing at attention as the camera pans slowly by. They play firemen—at least they're *dressed* that way.

★   ★   ★

The cheapest Stooges feature was *Gold Raiders* (1951). This one, featuring Shemp Howard, has the boys wreaking havoc on a western town. "*Gold Raiders* was an ultra-quickie," said Edward Bernds, the film's director, in a fan club publication. The movie was shot in a grand total of five days, at what Bernds terms "an unbelievably low price" ($50,000). The movie was independently produced, and released by United Artists.

★   ★   ★

The most expensive Stooges feature was *Snow White and the Three Stooges* (1961), budgeted at the then-unbelievable amount of $3 million-plus. *Snow White,* starring Carol Heiss, casts the Stooges as medieval medicine men sitting in for the Seven Dwarfs. In this one the dwarfs are on sabbatical, prospecting in King Solomon's mines. Unfortunately, the movie, which was shot in color, bombed at the box office. After this endeavor the Stooges began producing their own feature films with Norman Maurer as producer. These films, all budgeted at several hundred thousand dollars, reportedly earned handsome profits for their financial participants.

★   ★   ★

The last Three Stooges theatrical feature was *The Outlaws Is Coming* (1965), produced and directed by Norman

Maurer, who also provided the screen story. Elwood Ullman, a longtime Stooges scriptwriter, provided the screenplay, which has the boys sent out West to stop the killing of
buffalo. The film included uncharacteristically little violence, despite the fact that an old-fashioned shoot-out cli-
maxed the action.

★   ★   ★

In addition to their completed feature films, several other
projects were announced by the Stooges that never mate-
rialized. Shortly after the premiere of **Snow White and the
Three Stooges,** there was discussion of a **Pinocchio and the
Three Stooges.** There were plans for **The Three Stooges in
King Arthur's Court,** which also fell by the wayside. One
film announced as **The Three Stooges Meet the Space Men**
eventually emerged as **The Three Stooges in Orbit** (1962).
The use of the word "orbit" in the title was an attempted tie-
in with the publicity of the United States space program.

DÉJÀ STOOGE

Throughout their 25-year Columbia Pictures short subjects career, the Three Stooges produced 190 comedy films.
Many of these films, however, feature old footage from
earlier episodes. Some shorts rely heavily on old film, with
only a minimal amount of new material. All in all, about one
of every five Stooges shorts includes old footage.

Jules White, who produced the majority of the Stooges'
films, says this was an "economy measure" required by
Columbia Pictures' tiny short subjects budget. By the 1950s
the budgets were minuscule, and White was frequently
forced to dig up old footage to assemble "new" episodes.

Below is a list of the Columbia Stooges shorts that included considerable old footage.

With Curly Howard

1. *From Nurse to Worse* (1940). The traffic sequence from *Dizzy Doctors* (1937) is included in this episode.
2. *In the Sweet Pie and Pie* (1941). This one features the classic "dance lesson" scene from *Hoi Polloi* (1935).
3. *Dizzy Detectives* (1943). This film includes the carpentry sequence from *Pardon My Scotch* (1935).
4. *Dizzy Pilots* (1943). Part of the army training footage from *Boobs in Arms* (1940) turns up in this short.
5. *Beer Barrel Polecats* (1946). Footage featuring the Stooges as prisoners from two different films, *So Long Mr. Chumps* (1941) and *In the Sweet Pie and Pie*, comprises much of this entry.

With Shemp Howard

1. *Vagabond Loafers* (1949). This episode includes a number of scenes from *A Plumbing We Will Go* (1940).
2. *Merry Mavericks* (1951). Introductory footage from *Phony Express* (1943), dealing with a couple of supporting players, pops up in this short.
3. *Pest Man Wins* (1951). Pie-throwing footage from *In the Sweet Pie and Pie*, as well as *Half-Wits Holiday* (1947), is used in this episode.
4. *Up in Daisy's Penthouse* (1953). This film includes some footage from *Three Dumb Clucks* (1937).

Shemp Howard, solo performer, drops by
Columbia Pictures to visit his brothers on
the set of Pardon My Scotch (1935). Footage
from this short later turned up in Dizzy
Detectives (1943). (Photo courtesy of Babe
Howard.)

5. *Booty and the Beast* (1953). Footage from *Hold That Lion*
   (1947), dealing with a lion running loose on a moving train, is
   used.
6. *Loose Loot* (1953). Additional footage from *Hold That Lion*,
   concerning the Stooges' search for a swindler, is utilized.

7. *Tricky Dicks* (1953). More footage from *Hold That Lion,* dealing with the Stooges' problems closing a filing cabinet, turns up in this film.

8. *Rip, Sew and Stitch* (1953). Virtually the same episode as *Sing a Song of Six Pants* (1947), with minimal new material.

9. *Bubble Trouble* (1953). Most of the footage from the earlier *All Gummed Up* (1947) is used.

10. *Musty Musketeers* (1954). This short includes a good deal of film from *Fiddlers Three* (1948).

11. *Pals and Gals* (1954). Scenes from *Goofs and Saddles* (1937) and *Out West* (1947) are utilized.

12. *Knutzy Knights* (1954). This episode reworks the original plot line from *Squareheads of the Round Table* (1948), with much of its footage remaining intact.

13. *Scotched in Scotland* (1954). A remake of the earlier *Hot Scots* (1948), including virtually all of its "spooky castle" sequences.

14. *Fling in the Ring* (1955). This short includes most of the plot line, as well as footage, from *Fright Night* (1947).

15. *Of Cash and Hash* (1955). The majority of footage from *Shivering Sherlocks* (1948) is used.

16. *Bedlam in Paradise* (1955). Most of the film from *Heavenly Daze* (1948) is included in this entry.

17. *Stone Age Romeos* (1955). Film from *I'm a Monkey's Uncle* (1948) is used in this episode, with only a couple of new segments.

18. *Wham-Bam-Slam* (1955). Footage from *Pardon My Clutch* (1948) comprises most of this short.

19. *Hot Ice* (1955). Footage from two other movies, *Hot Scots* and *Crime on Their Hands* (1948), turns up in this one.

20. *Husbands Beware* (1956). The majority of sequences from *Brideless Groom* (1947) are used.

21. *Creeps* (1956). Footage from *The Ghost Talks* (1949) comprises almost all of this episode.

22. *Flagpole Jitters* (1956). A reworking of *Hokus Pokus* (1949), including most of its footage.

23. *For Crimin' Out Loud* (1956). A remake of *Who Done It?* (1949), featuring much of its original material.

24. *Rumpus in the Harem* (1956). This one includes a good deal of footage from *Malice in the Palace* (1949).
25. *Hot Stuff* (1956). This remake of *Fuelin' Around* (1949) includes most of its major sequences.
26. *Scheming Schemers* (1956). This short includes material from three different episodes: *A Plumbing We Will Go* (1940), *Half-Wits Holiday* (1947), and *Vagabond Loafers* (1949).
27. *Commotion on the Ocean* (1956). This film includes scenes from both *Crime on Their Hands* (1948) and *Dunked in the Deep* (1949).

With Joe Besser

1. *Guns a Poppin'* (1957). Footage from *Idiots Deluxe* (1945) comprises much of this entry.
2. *Rusty Romeos* (1957). This short, a reworking of *Corny Casanovas* (1952), also includes much of its footage.
3. *Fifi Blows Her Top* (1958). A couple of flashback sequences from *Love at First Bite* (1950) turns up in this one.
4. *Pies and Guys* (1958). The entire pie fight scene from *Half-Wits Holiday* (1947) comprises the climax of this episode.
5. *Oil's Well That Ends Well* (1958). The oil well scene from *Oily to Bed, Oily to Rise* (1939) is repeated in this film, along with some footage.
6. *Triple Crossed* (1959). The basic story line, as well as much of the footage, from *He Cooked His Goose* (1952) is included in this one.
7. *Sappy Bullfighters* (1959). Footage from the bull ring sequence of *What's the Matador?* (1942) is included in this episode.

THREE DIMENSIONAL STOOGES

When the 3-D craze swept the nation in the 1950s the Three Stooges jumped on the bandwagon. They turned out a couple of films in that process, as well as some 3-D comic books.

At Columbia Pictures Jules White, who produced the majority of the Stooges' short subjects, envisioned an entire series of Three Stooges films shot in 3-D. The first of these, **Spooks** (1953), was a standard haunted house adventure, with the boys as private eyes in search of a missing girl.

White followed this up with another 3-D episode, **Pardon My Backfire** (1953), which had the same kind of gags as the first entry. After this film, however, the 3-D idea was abandoned, as interest in that process was already beginning to die out.

The Three Stooges comic book series also featured some 3-D entries, which viewers could enjoy by wearing a special pair of glasses. But, like the 3-D movie gimmick, this idea was eventually abandoned.

THE STOOGE TUBE

Television actually made first-magnitude stars of the Three Stooges. Thanks to the release of their old movies to TV in 1958, the trio became overnight international celebrities. People who had never even seen the team in theaters were now enjoying them in the privacy of their own living rooms.

As vaudeville began to die out, the Stooges began appearing more frequently in nightclubs. They also popped up occasionally on television, and they popped out in a couple of 3-D comedies. (Photo courtesy of Babe Howard.)

The syndication of their old films to TV made enormous stars of the Three Stooges. Here they clown with Harry Fender, host of a local Stooges TV show in St. Louis, in the 1960s. (Photo courtesy of Harry Fender.)

In addition to their old movie reruns, the Stooges made three original television pilots, none of which were released to television in their original form.

★　　★　　★

The first Three Stooges TV pilot was produced at ABC Studios in Hollywood in the early 1950s. Supporting players included Emil Sitka and Symona Boniface, both of whom were Stooges movie regulars. Shemp Howard played the role of Third Stooge in this project, which included some gags from their Columbia movie series. For example, Emil Sitka remembers a scene in which the Stooges, playing wallpaper hangers, accidentally paper Sitka to a wall along with the wallpaper. This bit had been used in the Stooges short *A Bird in the Head* (1945), with Curly Howard.

★   ★   ★

The first color Stooges TV pilot was titled "Three Stooges Scrapbook," produced by Norman Maurer in 1960. Cast members included Emil Sitka and Cheerio Meredith, who also appeared in Stooges feature films. The pilot also included a laugh track and featured some reprises of original gags from their Columbia films. One gag, in which the Stooges crawl into bed with a hideous monster, was reworked from their 1948 short *Hot Scots,* featuring Shemp Howard. Footage from this pilot was reprocessed in black and white and used in the feature film *The Three Stooges in Orbit* (1962).

★   ★   ★

The last Stooges TV pilot was titled "Kooks Tour." This one, also filmed in color, was to be the initial entry in a travelogue series starring the Three Stooges. The pilot was again helmed by Norman Maurer. However, during production of the project, Larry Fine suffered a stroke, forcing him into retirement. The proposed series was scrapped, and, as this book goes to press, "Kooks Tour" has yet to be shown on television. It has, however, been sold in Super-8 format for home movie viewing and has also been seen at various private screenings.

GENUINELY COMIC BOOKS

One of the Stooges' most successful merchandising schemes was the Three Stooges comic book series. The first Three Stooges comics were published in 1949; the last were released in 1972. During this time more than 100 different editions were churned out, all bearing the likenesses of the Three Stooges.

★　　★　　★

The first series featured the character of Curly as Third Stooge. These came out in 1949 and were distributed by Jubilee Publishing. Two issues comprised the initial short-lived series, which was edited by Norman Maurer. Maurer, a commercial artist, was a talented craftsman who even appeared in some comic book issues via his own artwork.

★　　★　　★

The second comic book series began in 1953 and was published by St. John Publishing. St. John churned out 48 Shemp issues, some of which were produced in a three-dimensional effect. Norman Maurer and Joe Kubert shared editing chores on this series.

★　　★　　★

After the St. John series was discontinued in 1957 Dell Publishing began grinding out Stooges comics of their own. The Third Stooge in this series, which started in 1959 and lasted until 1972, was patterned after Joe DeRita. Issues often included a color photograph of the team on the cover. In addition, special editions were devoted entirely to their theatrical feature films, coinciding with the release of those films. These also featured publicity stills from the films.

HYSTERICAL DOCUMENTATION

In addition to the Stooges comic books, a handful of "Stoogeographies" have been published. Two of these involved original Stooge members as authors.

★　　★　　★

The first Stooges biography was *Stroke of Luck,* written by James Carone in collaboration with Larry Fine. During the planning stages of the book Larry was a resident of the Motion Picture Country Home in Woodland Hills, California. The book was published by Siena Publishing and was sold nationwide.

★　　★　　★

Moe Howard and the Three Stooges (1977) was written by Moe Howard with assistance from his daughter, Joan Maurer. Moe had been compiling his memoirs for some time prior to the actual transcription of the book, which was released after his death. The book was published by Citadel Press and is still being sold nationwide.

★　　★　　★

As this book goes to press, another Three Stooges biography, *The Three Stooges Scrapbook,* is reportedly ready for publication. The book was written by Joan Maurer and Greg and Jeff Lenburg.

★　　★　　★

The Stooge Chronicles by Jeffrey Forrester was compiled from interviews with the people who had worked with, lived with, or were acquainted with the Three Stooges. The book was published in 1981 and is currently available nationwide.

★　　★　　★

In addition to comic books and biographies, a Three Stooges poetry book, *Stoogism Anthology,* was published in 1977. The book, edited by Paul Fericano and published by Scarecrow Books, includes a handful of studio publicity stills, a little Stooges history, and, of course, a collection of "Stoogist" poems.

TRULY ANIMATED PERSONALITIES

The Three Stooges turned up as cartoon characters numerous times throughout their television careers.

★　　★　　★

The first Three Stooges cartoon series was titled the "New Three Stooges" (1965), a series of five-minute episodes sold to TV via syndication. The series was released by Heritage Productions. Norman Maurer produced the series, and Edward Bernds directed many of the segments. The episodes included brief live-action sequences starring the Stooges. In addition, the Stooges provided the voices for their own cartoon characterizations. To this day, the series is shown in various local markets throughout the country.

★　　★　　★

A Three Stooges cartoon series not involving the flesh-and-blood Stooges was CBS's "Robonic Stooges" episodes. The series was produced by Hanna-Barbera Productions, in collaboration with Norman Maurer Productions. The cartoons initially were aired on CBS Television in the late 1970s

Joe DeRita, Moe Howard, and Larry Fine
became immortalized as cartoon
characters in the 1960s. (Photo courtesy
of Stephen Cox.)

and, until recently, were still being carried by the network in reruns. The series featured the Stooges as robotlike super-heroes and used the voices of Paul Winchell, Joe Baker, and Frank Welker as the Stooges. Ross Martin contributed the voice of "000," the Stooges' boss.

STOOGED TO THE GILLS

Over the years the likenesses of the Three Stooges have popped up on innumerable kinds of consumer products—and, despite the fact that the Stooges themselves officially retired more than 10 years ago, the products continue to surface year after year.

In the 1930s collectors' items like hand puppets and film viewers bore the likenesses of the trio featuring Curly Howard.

After Shemp Howard joined the team in the 1940s, the merchandising continued. For example, a comic book se-ries featuring the Shemp character lasted for five years.

But the real flood of Three Stooges–themed products occurred in the 1950s, after the original Three Stooges movie comedies hit the TV market. By the 1960s there was an outpouring of such items as Three Stooges puppets, film viewers, comic books, question-and-answer boards, jigsaw puzzles, rubber stamps, costumes, punch-out boards, cut-out boards, "sticker" books, "erasable" books, coloring books, filmstrip projectors, plastic phonograph records, inflatable toys, plastic flicker rings, and board games, among other items.

A brand-new assortment of Stooges products is now available to the public: statuettes bearing the team's like-nesses, "limited edition" wall posters, movie poster stills, studio production stills, Super-8 films, VHS and Beta format videocassettes, T-shirts, and bumper stickers with Stooge-like verbal interpretations of such traditional phrases as, "Remind me to murder you later," and "I'm a victim of circumstance." These products are all available through the Official 3 Stooges Fan Club.

FANNING A REVIVAL

The original Three Stooges fan club was formed in the late 1950s. It was authorized by Norman Maurer Productions and headquartered in Hollywood, California. Members who joined the club received a letter from "Your pals, the Three Stooges," as well as some stamps bearing the team's likenesses, publicity photos of the group, and a handful of "official membership cards," among other items.

★　　★　　★

Another Three Stooges fan club was formed in the early 1970s. A young Chicagoan named Ralph Schiller contacted the Three Stooges themselves—Moe Howard, Larry Fine, and Joe DeRita—and they each gave Schiller the go-ahead for forming his own organization. Schiller put together the "Three Stooges Club," which has now been taken over by Moe Feinberg, Larry Fine's brother, of Philadelphia. Under Feinberg's leadership, the club publishes a bimonthly newsletter carrying newly discovered information about the Stooges, coverage of Stooges-themed activities, and advertisements for Stooges merchandise. Thousands of Three Stooges fanatics across the country are now members of the club.

★　　★　　★

These dedicated Chicago area fans enjoy aping their favorite Stooges (Photo courtesy of Sean McCool.)

The most recent Stooges club to surface is the Official 3 Stooges Fan Club. The club, according to its introductory newsletter, ". . . has been formed under the endorsement and authorization of Columbia Pictures Industries, Inc., and Norman Maurer Productions, Inc." The club devotes extensive newsletter space to advertisements for various Three Stooges–themed products, such as home videocassettes of the team's short subjects, publicity stills from their movies, and wall posters blown up from actual Stooges photographs.

EPILOGUE:
THE STOOGE PHENOMENON

Thanks to television, the Three Stooges have finally come into their own as America's favorite comedy team—and it's only taken half a century to do it.

It's sad to say, but the Three Stooges practically missed the boat in just about every career endeavor they attempted. They started their short subjects series at a time when shorts were decidedly on their way out. They began starring in feature films when their kind of movie, the slapstick farce, was no longer a staple of the movie industry. And by the time the Stooges began gaining momentum in the TV industry, the original members were well into their sixties.

Today the Three Stooges are more popular than they've ever been. Their ancient movies are packing 'em in at theaters. Their television ratings are higher than ever. And thousands of people are joining Stooges fan clubs.

True to form, the Stooges themselves are missing out again. It's the final chapter to the ironic career story of the Three Stooges. Today they're more popular than ever, and none of the original members are around to enjoy it. And that would seem to be the cruelest irony of all.

Yes, the Three Stooges missed the boat, all right. They missed the boat in just about every respect but one: they knew how to make people laugh. And they prove it every time one of their old movies is screened.

But will the Stooges be funny 50 years from now? Will audiences still laugh at their wild antics and roughhouse slapstick? Perhaps not. After all, physical comedy as we know it dates back centuries to the dawn of modern civilization.

And who's to say that kind of thing will last another 50 years?

APPENDIX:
THREE STOOGES FILMOGRAPHY

STARRING FEATURE FILMS

In 1945 the Three Stooges appeared in their first starring feature film. Following this initial effort, the Stooges received top billing in five more theatrical features. All of these films were released theatrically by Columbia and are listed below.

1. *Rockin' in the Rockies* (1945). Directed by Vernon Keayes. The boys try to help two aspiring actresses break into show business. Curly Howard plays the Third Stooge in this film. Running time: 63 minutes.

2. *Have Rocket, Will Travel* (1959). Directed by David Lowell Rich. The Stooges are space center custodians accidentally launched into outer space. This and subsequent films star Joe DeRita as the Third Stooge. Running time: 76 minutes.
3. *The Three Stooges Meet Hercules* (1962). Directed by Edward Bernds. The boys find themselves in Ancient Greece, where they encounter various mythical characters. Running time: 89 minutes.
4. *The Three Stooges in Orbit* (1962). Directed by Edward Bernds. Martians plan to invade Earth but, after observing the Stooges, decide to destroy it instead. Running time: 87 minutes.
5. *The Three Stooges Go Around the World in a Daze* (1963). Directed by Norman Maurer. An updated version of the classic Jules Verne story, with the Stooges accompanying the youngest member of the Fogg family around the globe. Running time: 94 minutes.
6. *The Outlaws Is Coming* (1965). Directed by Norman Maurer. The boys are sent out West to halt the slaughtering of bison. Running time: 89 minutes.

MISCELLANEOUS FEATURE FILMS

In addition to their starring vehicles, the Stooges appeared in 15 other feature films, in costarring, supporting, or "guest" roles. These films are listed below. The name of the studio that distributed the film follows year of release.

1. *Soup to Nuts* (1930). Fox. Directed by Benjamin Stoloff. Shemp Howard plays the Third Stooge in this film. Running time: 65 minutes.
2. *Turn Back the Clock* (1933). MGM. Directed by Edgar Selwyn. Curly Howard plays the Third Stooge in this and subsequent films. Running time: 80 minutes.
3. *Meet the Baron* (1933). MGM. Directed by Walter Lang. Running time: 67 minutes.

4. *Dancing Lady* (1933). MGM. Directed by Robert Z. Leonard. Running time: 82 minutes.
5. *Fugitive Lovers* (1934). MGM. Directed by Richard Boleslavsky. Running time: 84 minutes.
6. *Hollywood Party* (1934). MGM. Directed by Richard Boleslavsky. Running time: 70 minutes.
7. *The Captain Hates the Sea* (1934). Columbia. Directed by Lewis Milestone. Running time: 92 minutes.
8. *Start Cheering* (1938). Columbia. Directed by Albert S. Rogell. Running time: 78 minutes.
9. *Time Out for Rhythm* (1941). Columbia. Directed by Sidney Salkow. Running time: 74 minutes.
10. *My Sister Eileen* (1942). Columbia. Directed by Alexander Hall. Running time: 96 minutes.
11. *Swing Parade of 1946* (1946). Monogram. Directed by Phil Karlson. Running time: 73 minutes.
12. *Gold Raiders* (1951). United Artists. Directed by Edward Bernds. Shemp Howard plays the Third Stooge in this film. Running time: 56 minutes.
13. *Snow White and the Three Stooges* (1961). 20th Century–Fox. Directed by Walter Lang. Joe DeRita plays the Third Stooge in this and subsequent films. Running time: 107 minutes.
14. *It's a Mad Mad Mad Mad World* (1963). United Artists. Directed by Stanley Kramer. Running time: 192 minutes.
15. *Four for Texas* (1963). Warner Brothers. Directed by Robert Aldrich. Running time: 124 minutes.

STARRING SHORT SUBJECTS

In 1934 the Three Stooges signed with Columbia Pictures for appearances in a series of short subject comedy films. That series lasted 25 years.

Columbia kept its shorts department operating until 1958, when Harry Cohn, founder of the studio, died. With him died the shorts division, and the Stooges found themselves out of work. Columbia, however, continued to release the Stooges films to theaters well into 1959, completing 25 consecutive years of screen stoogery.

★   ★   ★

Altogether the Three Stooges starred in 190 short subjects at Columbia. Ninety-seven of them starred Curly Howard (numbers 1–97), 77 starred Shemp Howard (numbers 98–174), and 16 starred Joe Besser (numbers 175–190).

All of the films listed below are less than 20 minutes in length and were released theatrically by Columbia Pictures. These films comprised the "Three Stooges" series.

1. *Woman Haters* (1934). Directed by Archie Gottler. The boys are members of a "woman haters club" who find it difficult to keep their vows. This and subsequent films star Curly Howard as the Third Stooge.
2. *Punch Drunks* (1934). Directed by Lou Breslow. Curly goes crazy whenever he hears "Pop Goes the Weasel," so his partners decide to make a prizefighter out of him.
3. *Men in Black* (1934). Directed by Raymond McCarey. As doctors, the boys turn a hospital upside down with their bizarre behavior.
4. *Three Little Pigskins* (1934). Directed by Raymond McCarey. The Stooges are mistaken for a trio of college football players.
5. *Horse Collars* (1935). Directed by Clyde Bruckman. A group of western badmen hold a necktie party in the Stooges' honor.
6. *Restless Knights* (1935). Directed by Charles Lamont. The boys are sentenced to be executed when their queen is kidnapped.
7. *Pop Goes the Easel* (1935). Directed by Del Lord. The Stooges incite a wild clay-throwing riot in an art school.

8. *Uncivil Warriors* (1935). Directed by Del Lord. The boys are Union military experts who masquerade as Confederate officers.

9. *Pardon My Scotch* (1935). Directed by Del Lord. The boys concoct their own brand of liquor, which results in their attending a society dinner masquerading as distillers.

10. *Hoi Polloi* (1935). Directed by Del Lord. A wealthy professor tries to make gentlemen of the threesome, with disastrous results.

11. *Three Little Beers* (1935). Directed by Del Lord. The boys cause a traffic jam when a load of beer kegs spills out of their delivery truck.

12. *Ants in the Pantry* (1936). Directed by Preston Black. The Stooges are ordered by their boss to cook up some exterminating business.

13. *Movie Maniacs* (1936). Directed by Del Lord. The Stooges try to break into the movie business.

14. *Half Shot Shooters* (1936). Directed by Preston Black. The boys join the army and accidentally destroy several military installations.

15. *Disorder in the Court* (1936). Directed by Preston Black. The Stooges wreak havoc in a courtroom when they're called in to testify.

16. *A Pain in the Pullman* (1936). Directed by Preston Black. The boys are obnoxious train passengers.

17. *False Alarms* (1936). Directed by Del Lord. The boys are firemen who always manage to miss out on the fires.

18. *Whoops I'm an Indian* (1936). Directed by Del Lord. The Stooges are forced to disguise themselves as Indians to avoid the local sheriff.

19. *Slippery Silks* (1936). Directed by Preston Black. The boys start a pastry fight at a fashion show.

20. *Grips, Grunts and Groans* (1937). Directed by Preston Black. The Stooges are in trouble when a burly wrestler is knocked unconscious.

21. *Dizzy Doctors* (1937). Directed by Del Lord. The boys are modern-day medicine men who invade a hospital to sell their wares.

22. *Three Dumb Clucks* (1937). Directed by Del Lord. When the Stooges' father decides to marry a showgirl they attempt to stop the wedding.
23. *Back to the Woods* (1937). Directed by Preston Black. The boys- are pitiful pilgrims who raise the ire of some local Indians.
24. *Goofs and Saddles* (1937). Directed by Del Lord. The Stooges are assigned to track down a group of cattle thieves.
25. *Cash and Carry* (1937). Directed by Del Lord. The Stooges buy a "treasure map" from a pair of con men.
26. *Playing the Ponies* (1937). Directed by Charles Lamont. The Stooges decide to get into the racing business.
27. *The Sitter-Downers* (1937). Directed by Del Lord. The boys build their own house, with the expected slapstick results.
28. *Termites of 1938* (1938). Directed by Del Lord. The Stooges are pest exterminators who wind up entertaining at a party.
29. *Wee Wee Monsieur* (1938). Directed by Del Lord. The boys accidentally join the French Foreign Legion.
30. *Tassels in the Air* (1938). Directed by Charley Chase. The boys are painters who wreak havoc at a bridge party.
31. *Flat Foot Stooges* (1938). Directed by Charley Chase. The Stooges are firemen who bring their horses to a Turkish bath.
32. *Healthy, Wealthy and Dumb* (1938). Directed by Del Lord. The boys take up residence at a ritzy hotel.
33. *Violent Is the Word for Curly* (1938). Directed by Charley Chase. The Stooges are service station attendants mistaken for professors.
34. *Three Missing Links* (1938). Directed by Jules White. The boys go on location in Africa to shoot a movie.
35. *Mutts to You* (1938). Directed by Charley Chase. The boys, proprietors of an automatic dog laundry, are accused of kidnapping.
36. *Three Little Sew and Sews* (1939). Directed by Del Lord. The Stooges are tailors who become embroiled in an international spy plot.
37. *We Want Our Mummy* (1939). Directed by Del Lord. The boys

decide to disguise Curly as a mummy in order to thwart a gang of crooks.

38. *A-Ducking They Did Go* (1939). Directed by Del Lord. The Stooges are vagrants who find work selling phony hunting club memberships.

39. *Yes We Have No Bonanza* (1939). Directed by Del Lord. The boys dig for gold but come up with bonds instead.

40. *Saved by the Belle* (1939). Directed by Charley Chase. The Stooges become involved in a plot to overthrow a government.

41. *Calling All Curs* (1939). Directed by Jules White. The boys run an animal hospital—complete with beds for the "patients."

42. *Oily to Bed, Oily to Rise* (1939). Directed by Jules White. The trio discovers an oil well, which Curly must sit on to contain.

43. *Three Sappy People* (1939). Directed by Jules White. The boys masquerade as a trio of eminent psychiatrists.

44. *You Nazty Spy* (1940). Directed by Jules White. The Stooges are put in charge of running a country.

45. *Rockin' Through the Rockies* (1940). Directed by Jules White. Traveling across the country in a covered wagon, the Stooges are faced with a snowstorm, lack of food, and other obstacles.

46. *A-Plumbing We Will Go* (1940). Directed by Del Lord. The boys pretend to be plumbers to escape the police.

47. *Nutty But Nice* (1940). Directed by Jules White. The Stooges are entertainers who try to help out a depressed little girl.

48. *How High Is Up?* (1940). Directed by Del Lord. The boys are hired as construction workers.

49. *From Nurse to Worse* (1940). Directed by Jules White. Curly pretends he's mentally ill so the Stooges can swindle an insurance company.

50. *No Census, No Feeling* (1940). Directed by Del Lord. The boys are tramps who find work as census takers.

51. *Cookoo Cavaliers* (1940). Directed by Jules White. The Stooges are beginning beauticians who cause three showgirls to lose their hair.

52. *Boobs in Arms* (1940). Directed by Jules White. Our three soldiers become intoxicated with laughing gas.
53. *So Long, Mr. Chumps* (1941). Directed by Jules White. The boys search for an "honest man," resulting in their going to prison for assaulting a policeman.
54. *Dutiful but Dumb* (1941). Directed by Del Lord. The Stooges, photographers on assignment in a foreign country, find themselves in front of a firing squad.
55. *All the World's a Stooge* (1941). Directed by Del Lord. The boys disguise themselves as children in order to avoid arrest.
56. *I'll Never Heil Again* (1941). Directed by Jules White. The Stooges, in charge of a mythical government, call a summit meeting with their allies.
57. *An Ache in Every Stake* (1941). Directed by Del Lord. The boys are icemen trying to make a delivery on a very hot day.
58. *In the Sweet Pie and Pie* (1941). Directed by Jules White. The Stooges marry three society heiresses, who scheme to get rid of them.
59. *Some More of Samoa* (1941). Directed by Del Lord. The boys encounter a tribe of cannibals.
60. *Loco Boy Makes Good* (1942). Directed by Jules White. Curly makes a spectacle of himself on the dance floor when the Stooges entertain at a nightclub.
61. *Cactus Makes Perfect* (1942). Directed by Del Lord. The trio discovers a lost mine with Curly's gold-finding machine.
62. *What's the Matador?* (1942). Directed by Jules White. In Mexico the boys raise the ire of a jealous man.
63. *Matri-Phony* (1942). Directed by Harry Edwards. In ancient times the Stooges try to pass Curly off as a "redhead" to an extremely nearsighted emperor.
64. *Three Smart Saps* (1942). Directed by Jules White. The boys must get into prison to break their future father-in-law out.
65. *Even as I.O.U.* (1942). Directed by Del Lord. The boys buy what they think is a talking race horse.
66. *Sock-a-Bye Baby* (1942). Directed by Jules White. The three bachelors become foster fathers when a baby is abandoned on their doorstep.

67. *They Stooge to Conga* (1942). Directed by Del Lord. The boys find themselves in a nest of enemy spies.
68. *Dizzy Detectives* (1943). Directed by Jules White. When an "ape man" is thought to be behind a rash of burglaries, it's up to the Stooges to catch him.
69. *Spook Louder* (1943). Directed by Del Lord. The boys encounter a trio of spies dressed as spooky characters.
70. *Back from the Front* (1943). Directed by Jules White. The Stooges find themselves aboard a ship full of Nazis, so they disguise themselves as Nazis.
71. *Three Little Twirps* (1943). Directed by Harry Edwards. The boys are in trouble with the management of a traveling circus.
72. *Higher Than a Kite* (1943). Directed by Del Lord. The Stooges are garage mechanics who find themselves in a bomb being dropped over enemy territory!
73. *I Can Hardly Wait* (1943). Directed by Jules White. Curly has a bad tooth, and it's driving his partners crazy.
74. *Dizzy Pilots* (1943). Directed by Jules White. The trio designs a new type of airplane that's so wide that they can't get it out of their hangar.
75. *Phony Express* (1943). Directed by Del Lord. The boys are vagrants mistaken for a trio of tough lawmen.
76. *A Gem of a Jam* (1943). Directed by Del Lord. The Stooges play custodians who run afoul of bank robbers.
77. *Crash Goes the Hash* (1944). Directed by Jules White. The three ruffians invade a society party and serve a cooked turkey with a live parrot inside.
78. *Busy Buddies* (1944). Directed by Del Lord. The boys go through a series of schemes to raise some money to pay their bills.
79. *The Yoke's on Me* (1944). Directed by Jules White. The Stooges buy a farm, complete with such traditional livestock as an ostrich.
80. *Idle Roomers* (1944). Directed by Del Lord. The boys are bellhops who encounter a vicious monster in one of the rooms.

81. *Gents without Cents* (1945). Directed by Jules White. The Stooges are unemployed comedians trying to get a break in show business.

82. *No Dough, Boys* (1945). Directed by Jules White. The boys pretend to be a Japanese acrobatic trio when they stumble upon a German spy ring.

83. *Three Pests in a Mess* (1945). Directed by Del Lord. Curly thinks he has accidentally killed a man, so the Stooges bring the "body" (a mannequin) to a deserted graveyard to bury it.

84. *Booby Dupes* (1945). Directed by Del Lord. The boys are suckered into buying a broken-down fishing boat.

85. *Idiots Deluxe* (1945). Directed by Jules White. When the Stooges go on a hunting trip their car is stolen by a bear.

86. *If a Body Meets a Body* (1945). Directed by Jules White. The boys are forced to spend the night in a spooky old mansion, solving a mystery in the process.

87. *Micro-Phonies* (1945). Directed by Edward Bernds. The boys, pretending to be singers, "perform" at a society recital.

88. *Beer Barrel Polecats* (1946). Directed by Jules White. Our three beer barons wind up in prison.

89. *A Bird in the Head* (1946). Directed by Edward Bernds. The Stooges, wallpaper hangers, tangle with a mad doctor.

90. *Uncivil Warbirds* (1946). Directed by Jules White. The Stooges are southern gents involved in the War Between the States.

91. *The Three Troubledoers* (1946). Directed by Edward Bernds. The boys become law officers in a western town with a high mortality rate for public officials.

92. *Monkey Businessmen* (1946). Directed by Edward Bernds. The Stooges enroll in a sanitarium for a little rest.

93. *Three Loan Wolves* (1946). Directed by Jules White. A baby boy is abandoned at the trio's pawn shop.

94. *G.I. Wanna Home* (1946). Directed by Jules White. Returning home from military service, our three veterans can't find a place to live.

95. *Rhythm and Weep* (1946). Directed by Jules White. The boys

are musicians who contemplate suicide when they're fired from their jobs.

96. *Three Little Pirates* (1946). Directed by Edward Bernds. The Stooges don disguises to escape a tyrannical ruler but wind up in a den of pirates.
97. *Half-Wits Holiday* (1947). Directed by Jules White. A professor believes he can change the Stooges' crude ways and make gentlemen of them.
98. *Fright Night* (1947). Directed by Edward Bernds. The boys are fight managers in trouble with a gang of mobsters. This and subsequent films star Shemp Howard as Third Stooge.
99. *Out West* (1947). Directed by Edward Bernds. Shemp has an ailing leg, so his partners take him on a vacation out West.
100. *Hold That Lion* (1947). Directed by Jules White. The Stooges encounter a live lion while on a train trip.
101. *Brideless Groom* (1947). Directed by Edward Bernds. The boys must find Shemp a wife in order to collect a fortune.
102. *Sing a Song of Six Pants* (1947). Directed by Jules White. The Stooges are tailors in trouble with a gang of bank robbers.
103. *All Gummed Up* (1947). Directed by Jules White. The boys eat a "marshmallow jumbo" cake—only they used bubble gum instead of marshmallows.
104. *Shivering Sherlocks* (1948). Directed by Del Lord. The Stooges are chased by a huge hunchback while investigating a creepy old house.
105. *Pardon My Clutch* (1948). Directed by Edward Bernds. While loading up their car for a camping trip the boys encounter all sorts of problems.
106. *Squareheads of the Round Table* (1948). Directed by Edward Bernds. The boys are traveling entertainers in Merrie Olde England, who try to thwart an assassination plot.
107. *Fiddlers Three* (1948). Directed by Jules White. The Stooges are court comedians who help their king recover his kidnapped daughter.
108. *Heavenly Daze* (1948). Directed by Jules White. Shemp

dreams that he has died and returned to Earth to haunt his partners.

109. *Hot Scots* (1948). Directed by Edward Bernds. The boys masquerade as Scotsmen to get a job as detectives in an old Scottish castle.

110. *I'm a Monkey's Uncle* (1948). Directed by Jules White. The Stooges are cavemen whose girlfriends are stolen.

111. *Mummy's Dummies* (1948). Directed by Edward Bernds. The boys become royal chamberlains in ancient Egypt.

112. *Crime on Their Hands* (1948). Directed by Edward Bernds. The trio are custodians who want to become reporters.

113. *The Ghost Talks* (1949). Directed by Jules White. The Stooges encounter everything from invisible ghosts to talking skeletons in a haunted castle.

114. *Who Done It?* (1949). Directed by Edward Bernds. A wealthy old man disappears, so the Stooges—as private eyes—try to find him.

115. *Hokus Pokus* (1949). Directed by Jules White. The boys fall under the influence of a hypnotist.

116. *Fuelin' Around* (1949). Directed by Edward Bernds. The Stooges are kidnapped by foreign spies when they're mistaken for an eminent professor and his assistants.

117. *Malice in the Palace* (1949). Directed by Jules White. The Stooges are restauranteurs in search of a rare diamond.

118. *Vagabond Loafers* (1949). Directed by Edward Bernds. The boys are plumbers accused of thievery.

119. *Dunked in the Deep* (1949). Directed by Jules White. The boys are unwilling stowaways on a freighter.

120. *Punchy Cowpunchers* (1950). Directed by Edward Bernds. The Stooges are assigned to bring in a gang of dreaded desperadoes.

121. *Hugs and Mugs* (1950). Directed by Jules White. The boys become involved with a gang of female gem thieves.

122. *Dopey Dicks* (1950). Directed by Edward Bernds. A mad scientist traps the Stooges in a creepy old mansion, complete with runaway robot.

123. *Love at First Bite* (1950). Directed by Jules White. The trio tells of how they met their fiancées in Europe.

124. *Self Made Maids* (1950). Directed by Jules White. The boys want to marry their girlfriends, even though the girls' dad objects.

125. *Three Hams on Rye* (1950). Directed by Jules White. The Stooges are stagehands hoping to get a break as actors.

126. *Studio Stoops* (1950). Directed by Edward Bernds. The boys are pest exterminators mistaken for movie studio publicists.

127. *Slaphappy Sleuths* (1950). Directed by Jules White. The Stooges are detectives on the lookout for a gang of service station robbers.

128. *A Snitch in Time* (1950). Directed by Edward Bernds. The boys get in the way of a gang of criminals, resulting in a wild free-for-all.

129. *Three Arabian Nuts* (1950). Directed by Edward Bernds. Shemp finds a lamp with a genie in it, causing problems for him and his partners.

130. *Baby Sitters' Jitters* (1951). Directed by Jules White. The boys try their luck as professional baby-sitters, and wind up reuniting a separated couple.

131. *Don't Throw That Knife* (1951). Directed by Jules White. The Stooges incur the wrath of a jealousy-crazed knife thrower.

132. *Scrambled Brains* (1951). Directed by Jules White. Shemp, who is having hallucinations, is put in the care of his partners.

133. *Merry Mavericks* (1951). Directed by Edward Bernds. The boys spend a night in a spooky old house, full of crooks disguising themselves as ghosts.

134. *The Tooth Will Out* (1951). Directed by Edward Bernds. The boys enroll in dentistry school.

135. *Hula-La-La* (1951). Directed by Hugh McCollum. The Stooges almost wind up as part of a shrunken head collection when they journey to a tropical island.

136. *Pest Man Wins* (1951). Directed by Jules White. The boys are pest exterminators who provoke a wild pie fight at a society party.

137. *A Missed Fortune* (1952). Directed by Jules White. The Stooges encounter a trio of "wealthy widows" who think the boys are rich.

138. *Listen, Judge* (1952). Directed by Edward Bernds. The boys act as servants at a party and wind up covering virtually all of the guests with cake.
139. *Corny Casanovas* (1952). Directed by Jules White. All three Stooges are engaged to the same woman.
140. *He Cooked His Goose* (1952). Directed by Jules White. The boys are the principal players in a marital mix-up.
141. *Gents in a Jam* (1952). Directed by Edward Bernds. Shemp's rich uncle decides to pay the Stooges a visit.
142. *Three Dark Horses* (1952). Directed by Jules White. The boys are custodians who become caught up in the excitement of an election.
143. *Cookoo on a Choochoo* (1952). Directed by Jules White. The Stooges practice their mayhem aboard a derailed train car.
144. *Up in Daisy's Penthouse* (1953). Directed by Jules White. The Stooges' dad decides to get married, but his girlfriend winds up marrying Shemp.
145. *Booty and the Beast* (1953). Directed by Jules White. The boys chase a man aboard a moving train in order to retrieve some stolen bonds.
146. *Loose Loot* (1953). Directed by Jules White. A man gyps the Stooges out of their inheritance.
147. *Tricky Dicks* (1953). Directed by Jules White. The boys are policemen ordered to track down a murderer.
148. *Spooks* (1953). Directed by Jules White. The Stooges are private eyes who masquerade as pie salesmen to find a missing girl.
149. *Pardon My Backfire* (1953). Directed by Jules White. The boys tangle with some criminals when they agree to repair their stolen car.
150. *Rip, Sew and Stitch* (1953). Directed by Jules White. The Stooges are tailors about to be dispossessed.
151. *Bubble Trouble* (1953). Directed by Jules White. The boys invent a formula that turns an old man into an ape.
152. *Goof on the Roof* (1953). Directed by Jules White. Shemp tries to install a television antenna and winds up falling through the ceiling on top of his partners.
153. *Income Tax Sappy* (1954). Directed by Jules White. The boys

are in trouble with the government for falsifying income tax returns.

154. *Musty Musketeers* (1954). Directed by Jules White. The Stooges can't get married until the royal princess is wed.

155. *Pals and Gals* (1954). Directed by Jules White. The boys help a trio of girls when a crook holds their father prisoner.

156. *Knutzy Knights* (1954). Directed by Jules White. In medieval times the Stooges help reunite two lovers.

157. *Shot in the Frontier* (1954). Directed by Jules White. The Stooges are forced into a showdown by three bad guys.

158. *Scotched in Scotland* (1954). Directed by Jules White. The boys graduate from detective school—with the lowest possible honors—and are assigned to a case in an old castle.

159. *Fling in the Ring* (1955). Directed by Jules White. Some gangsters plan to bump off the Stooges in a deserted warehouse.

160. *Of Cash and Hash* (1955). Directed by Jules White. The Stooges are accused of holding up an armored car.

161. *Gypped in the Penthouse* (1955). Directed by Jules White. The boys all have problems with the same conniving woman.

162. *Bedlam in Paradise* (1955). Directed by Jules White. Shemp dreams that his partners have fallen under the influence of the devil.

163. *Stone Age Romeos* (1955). Directed by Jules White. The Stooges attempt to swindle a museum curator by selling him a movie featuring phony "cavemen."

164. *Wham-Bam-Slam* (1955). Directed by Jules White. The threesome decide to go on a camping trip.

165. *Hot Ice* (1955). Directed by Jules White. Working for Scotland Yard, the Stooges pursue a gang of diamond thieves.

166. *Blunder Boys* (1955). Directed by Jules White. The trio are police detectives threatened with dismissal unless they can catch a slippery crook.

167. *Husbands Beware* (1956). Directed by Jules White. Shemp marries off his portly sisters to his partners.

168. *Creeps*)1956). Directed by Jules White. The Stooges tell their kids a spooky bedtime story.

169. *Flagpole Jitters* (1956). Directed by Jules White. The boys

are bill posters at a theater who find themselves dancing on a flagpole.

170. *For Crimin' Out Loud* (1956). Directed by Jules White. The Stooges are assigned to protect a wealthy councilman and wind up tangling with a murderous gang of crooks.

171. *Rumpus in the Harem* (1956). Directed by Jules White. The boys have to raise some money to get their girlfriends out of slavery.

172. *Hot Stuff* (1956). Directed by Jules White. The trio are secret agents abducted by foreign spies.

173. *Scheming Schemers* (1956). Directed by Jules White. The boys are plumbers who instigate a pie-throwing fracas at a society party.

174. *Commotion on the Ocean* (1956). Directed by Jules White. The Stooges, in search of enemy spies, unwittingly aid one in stealing some top secret government data.

175. *Hoofs and Goofs* (1957). Directed by Jules White. In a dream sequence the Stooges' sister is reincarnated as a horse. This and subsequent films star Joe Besser as Third Stooge.

176. *Muscle Up a Little Closer* (1957). Directed by Jules White. The Stooges search for a stolen diamond ring, climaxing in a wild wrestling match.

177. *A Merry Mix Up* (1957). Directed by Jules White. The Stooges and two sets of lookalike brothers all converge at the same restaurant.

178. *Space Ship Sappy* (1957). Directed by Jules White. The boys travel to a planet inhabited by beautiful—but deadly—Amazons.

179. *Guns a Poppin'* (1957). Directed by Jules White. A wanted criminal makes life difficult for the Stooges during a vacation trip.

180. *Horsing Around* (1957). Directed by Jules White. The boys try to save a circus horse from being exterminated.

181. *Rusty Romeos* (1957). Directed by Jules White. Each of the Stooges decides to call on his girlfriend—and they all end up in the same apartment.

182. *Outer Space Jitters* (1957). Directed by Jules White. The

boys relate a fantastic story concerning space travel, a bizarre planet, and a plot to take over Earth with an army of monsters.
183. *Quiz Whiz* (1958). Directed by Jules White. After Joe wins a small fortune, and subsequently loses it, the Stooges must come up with the tax money.
184. *Fifi Blows Her Top* (1958). Directed by Jules White. The boys reminisce about their old flames.
185. *Pies and Guys* (1958). Directed by Jules White. A professor loses a bet that he can transform the three nitwits into gentlemen.
186. *Sweet and Hot* (1958). Directed by Jules White. Joe's sister, Tiny, has a psychological problem, so the Stooges try to help her out.
187. *Flying Saucer Daffy* (1958). Directed by Jules White. Joe wins a contest for his partners, but they refuse to share the winnings with him.
188. *Oil's Well That Ends Well* (1958). Directed by Jules White. The Stooges discover a flourishing oil well on their father's property.
189. *Triple Crossed* (1959). Directed by Jules White. The Stooges are at odds with each other because of some suspected philandering.
190. *Sappy Bullfighters* (1959). Directed by Jules White. The boys bring their comedy matador act south of the border.

MISCELLANEOUS SHORT SUBJECTS

Prior to their Columbia short subjects series the Stooges supported Ted Healy in a handful of MGM shorts. All of these films listed below are less than 20 minutes in length, and all were released theatrically by MGM.

1. *Nertsery Rhymes* (1933)
2. *Beer and Pretzels* (1933)
3. *Hello Pop* (1933)
4. *Plane Nuts* (1933)
5. *The Big Idea* (1934)

INDEX

A

Abbott and Costello, 16, 27
Ache in Every Stake, An, 114
A-Ducking They Did Go, 113
A-Plumbing We Will Go, 66, 90, 93
Adler, Felix, 58
Africa Screams, 27
Aherne, Brian, 86
Aldrich, Robert, 109
All Gummed Up, 92, 117
All the World's a Stooge, 65, 114
American Film, 24
Ants in the Pantry, 66, 111

B

Baby Sitters' Jitters, 119
Back from the Front, 115
Back to the Woods, 112
Backhand slap, 74, *illus.* 74
Baker, Joe, 102
Ball, Lucille, 41
Bank Dick, The, 26
Bedlam in Paradise, 92, 121
Beer and Pretzels, 124
Beer Barrel Polecats, 66, 90, 116
Bernds, Edward, 4, 12–13, 20–23, 45, 72, 88, 100, 108–9, 116–20, *illus.* 23

Besser, Joe, 14–15, *illus.* 15, 26
Big Idea, The, 124
Bird in the Head, A, 66, 97, 116
Black, Preston, 111–12
Blocker, Dan, 43
Blunder Boys, 121
Boleslavsky, Richard, 109
Boniface, Symona, 97
Boobs in Arms, 65, 90, 114
Booby Dupes, 55, 116
Booty and the Beast, 65, 91, 120
Bowery Boys, 22–23
Breen, Hurley, 43
Brennan, Walter, 41
Breslow, Lou, 110
Brideless Groom, 43, 92, 117
Bridges, Lloyd, 43
Bruckman, Clyde, 110
Bubble Trouble, 92, 120
Busy Buddies, 115

C

Cactus Makes Perfect, 66, 114
Callahan, Joe, 27
Calling All Curs, 113
Candy, John, ix, 47
Capra, Frank, 22
Captain Hates the Sea, The, 109
Carone, James, 99
Cartoon series, 100, *illus.* 101
Cash and Carry, 112
Chain-reaction punch, 80–81, *illus.* 80–81
Chase, Charley, 112–13
Cohn, Harry, 22, 109
Commotion on the Ocean, 45, 93, 122

Cookoo Cavaliers, 113
Cookoo on a Choochoo, 120
Corny Casanovas, 93, 120
Costello, Lou, 16, 131
Crash Goes the Hash, 33, 65, 115
Creeps, 92, 121
Crime on Their Hands, 66, 92–93, 118
Crosby, Bing, 18

D

Daily Variety, 24
Dancing Lady, 109
Dent, Vernon, 35–37, 56
DeRita, Joe, 16–17, 29–30
"DeRita Sisters and Junior," 18
"Dirty Larry, Dirty Moe, and Dirty Curly," 24
Disorder in the Court, 111
Dizzy Detectives, 90, 115
Dizzy Doctors, 90, 111
Dizzy Pilots, 90, 115
Don't Throw That Knife, 119
Dopey Dicks, 118
Double cheek slap, 73, *illus.* 73
Dunked in the Deep, 93, 118
Dutiful But Dumb, 66, 114

E

Ear twists, 70
Edwards, Harry, 114–15
Even As I.O.U., 114
Expression parodies, 66–67
Eye pokes, 70

F

Face slapping, 69, 72
False Alarms, 111
Fan clubs, 103

Feinberg, Joseph, 5
Feinberg, Louis, 4
Fericano, Paul, 100
Fiddlers Three, 92, 117
Fields, W. C., 26
Fifi Blows Her Top, 93, 123
Fighter's dance, 53–55
Fine, Larry, 4–5, *illus.* 6
Flagpole Jitters, 92, 121
Flat Foot Stooges, 112
Fling in the Ring, 92, 121
Flying Saucer Daffy, 40, 123
For Crimin' Out Loud, 67, 92, 122
Forehead slap, 75, *illus.* 75
Forrester, Jeffrey, 99
Four for Texas, 109
Frank, Gertrude "Babe," 12
"Fridays," 46
Fright Night, 92, 117
From Nurse to Worse, 66, 90, 113
Frome, Milton, 56
Fuelin' Around, 93, 118
Fugitive Lovers, 109

G

Garner, Mousie, 29, 31
Gem of a Jam, A, 115
Gents in a Jam, 38, 120
Gents without Cents, 116
Ghost Talks, The, 92, 118
G.I. Wanna Home, 116
Gift of Gab, 29
Givot, George, 27
Gold Raiders, 88, 109
Goof on the Roof, 120
Goofs and Saddles, 92, 112
Gorcey, Leo, 22–23
Gottler, Archie, 110
Great Movie Shorts, The, 52

Grips, Grunts and Groans, 62, 66, 111
Guns a Poppin', 93, 122
Gypped in the Penthouse, 121

H

Hair ripping, 70
Haircuts of the Stooges, 67–69, *illus.* 68
Hakins, Dick, 28–29, 31
Half Shot Shooters, 35, 111
Half-Wits Holiday, 8, 40, 56, 63, 90, 93, 117
Hall, Alexander, 109
Hall, Huntz, 22
Hand-to-hand head clunk, 82–83, *illus.* 82–83
Haney, Mabel, 4–5
"Haney Sisters and Fine," 5
Harling, Jack, 29
Have Rocket, Will Travel, 108
He Cooked His Goose, 93, 120
Healthy, Wealthy and Dumb, 66, 112
Healy, Ted, 1, 12, 19, 29, 67, 69, 72, 78, 85–86
Heavenly Daze, 92, 117
Heiss, Carol, 88
Hello Pop, 124
Herbert, Hugh, 51–52
Higher Than a Kite, 115
Hoi Polloi, 56–58, 90, 111
Hokus Pokus, 92, 118
Hold That Lion, 8, 66, 91–92, 117
Hollywood Party, 109
Holmes, Harry, 56
Hoofs and Goofs, 122
Horses Collars, 59, 110
Horsing Around, 122

Horwitz, Harry, 2
Horwitz, Jerome, 7
Horwitz, Sam, 12
Hot Ice, 92, 121
Hot Scots, 64, 92, 97, 118
Hot Stuff, 45, 93, 122
How High Is Up?, 113
Howard, Babe, 5–7, 13–14, 26
Howard, Curly, 7–8, *illus.* 9, 91
Howard, Helen, 58
Howard, Irving, 1
Howard, Jack, 1
Howard, Moe, 2, *illus.* 3
Howard, Shemp, 12, *illus.* 13, 25
Howard Furniture Company, 2
Hugs and Mugs, 118
Hula-La-La, 119
Husbands Beware, 92, 121

I

I Can Hardly Wait, 115
I'm a Monkey's Uncle, 118
I'll Never Heil Again, 66, 114
Idiots Deluxe, 93, 116
Idle Roomers, 64, 115
If a Body Meets a Body, 116
In the Sweet Pie and Pie, 63, 90, 114
Income Tax Sappy, 120
It's a Mad Mad Mad Mad World, 88, 109

J

"Jacques O'Mahoney," 43
Jamison, Bud, 33–34

K

Karlson, Phil, 109
Kascier, Johnny, 43
Kay, Erna, 14, 16
Keayes, Vernon, 107
Knutzy Knights, 35, 92, 121
"Kooks Tours," 97
Kramer, Stanley, 88, 109
Kubert, Joe, 98

L

Lamond, Don, 24
Lamont, Charles, 110, 112
Lang, Walter, 108–9
Laughton, Eddie, 31
Lenburg, Greg and Jeff, 99
Leonard, Robert Z., 109
Lewis, Jerry, 31
Lip quiver, 52
Listen Judge, 120
Literary parodies, 65
Loco Boy Makes Good, 66, 114
Loose Loot, 91, 120
Lord, Del, 20–21, 45, 110–17, *illus.* 21
Love at First Bite, 66, 93, 118
Loyola University football team, 44

M

Mahoney, Jock, 43
Malice in the Palace, 93, 118
Maltin, Leonard, 49, 52, 65
Mangean, Teddy, 43
Martin, Ross, 102
Matri-Phony, 114
Maurer, Jeffrey, 24

Maurer, Joan, 24, 99
Maurer, Michael, 24
Maurer, Norman, 24, 46,
   88–89, 97–98, 100, 108
McCarey, Raymond, 110
McCollum, Hugh, 119
Meet the Baron, 108
Men in Black, 65, 110
Meredith, Cheerio, 97
Merry Mavericks, 90, 119
Merry Mix Up, A, 45, 122
Micro-Phonies, 22, 46, 116
Milestone, Lewis, 109
Miller, Skins, 29
Minsky, Harold, 18
Missed Fortune, A, 119
Mitchell, Frank, 29–30, 43
*Moe Howard and the Three
   Stooges,* 99
Monkey Businessmen, 116
Motion Picture Country
   Home, 7, 99
Movie Comedy Teams, 65
Movie Maniacs, 111
Movie parodies, 65
Mummy's Dummies, 118
Muscle Up a Little Closer, 66,
   122
Musty Musketeers, 92, 121
Mutts to You, 33, 66, 112
My Sister Eileen, 86, 109

N

Nertsery Rhymes, 124
Neuman, Valerie, 7, 10
"New Three Stooges," 29–30,
   100, *illus.* 30
"Night and Day," 29
No Census, No Feeling, 50,
   113

No Dough Boys, 116
Norman Maurer Productions,
   46, 103–4
Nose tweak, 79, *illus.* 79
Nutty But Nice, 65, 113

O

Of Cash and Hash, 92, 121
Official 3 Stooges Fan Club,
   103–4
Oil's Well That Ends Well, 65,
   93, 123
Oily to Bed, Oily to Rise, 66,
   93, 113
Original television movies,
   96–97
Orville Knapp Band, 8
Out West, 43, 92, 117
Outer Space Jitters, 43, 112
Outlaws Is Coming, The, 88,
   108

P

A Pain in the Pullman, 111
Palma, Joe, 44
Pals and Gals, 92, 121
Pardon My Backfire, 94, 120
Pardon My Clutch, 92, 117
Pardon My Scotch, 66, 90,
   111
Pest Man Wins, 63, 67, 90,
   119
Phony Express, 90, 115
Pie throwing, 62–63
Pies and Guys, 56, 63, 93, 123
*Pinocchio and the Three
   Stooges,* 89
Plane Nuts, 124
Playing the Ponies, 112

Poke in the eyes, 76, *illus.* 77
Pop Goes the Easel, 21, 66,
  110
Porter, Cole, 29
Punch Drunks, 59, 110
Punchy Cowpunchers, 118

Q

Quiz Whiz, 123

R

Restless Knights, 110
Rhythm and Weep, 56, 66, 116
Rich, David Lowell, 108
"Rich Little Show," 46
Rip, Sew and Stitch, 92, 120
Roarke, John, 46
"Robonic Stooges," 100–102
Rockin' in the Rockies, 86,
  107
Rodentophobia, 59
Rogell, Albert S., 109
Rumpus in the Harem, 45, 93,
  122
Russell, Rosiland, 86
Rusty Romeos, 93, 122

S

Salkow, Sidney, 109
Sanborn, Fred, 86
Sappy Bullfighters, 93, 123
Saved by the Belle, 66, 113
Say One for Me, 16
"Saying Goodbye to Love," 29
Scentophobia, 62
Scheming Schemers, 45, 93,
  122
Schiller, Ralph, 103

Schonberger, Helen, 2
Scotched in Scotland, 92, 121
Scrambled Brains, 119
"Second City Television,"
  46–47
Self-Made Maids, 119
Selwyn, Edgar, 108
Sennett, Mack, 20
Sherman, Sam, 40
Shivering Sherlocks, 92, 117
Shot in the Frontier, 121
Shoulder spin, 52
Sing a Song of Six Pants, 66,
  92, 117
Sitka, Emil, 13, 37, 41, 97,
  illus. 38–39
Sitter-Downers, The, 112
Slaphappy Sleuths, 119
Slippery Silks, 50, 62, 111
Snitch in Time, A, 66, 119
*Snow White and the Three
  Stooges,* 88–89, 109
So Long, Mr. Chumps, 65, 90,
  114
Sock-a-Bye Baby, 66, 114
Some More of Samoa, 114
Song parodies, 66
Sound effects, 69–70
Soup to Nuts, 85, 108
Space Ship Sappy, 122
Spook Louder, 115
Spooks, 94, 120
*Squareheads of the
  Roundtable,* 92, 117
Start Cheering, 109
Stoloff, Benjamin, 108
Stomach punches, 70
Stone Age Romeos, 92, 121
Stooge Chronicles, The, 99
"Stoogeographies," 99
Stoogism Anthology, 100

Stripes, 47
Stroke of Luck, 99
Studio Stoops, 119
Sullivan, Jean, 16, 118
Sweet and Hot, 123
Swing Parade of 1946, 109

T

Tassels in the Air, 67, 112
"Ted Healy and His Stooges,"
   1, 2, 5, 8, 27–28, illus. 28
Television and the Three
   Stooges, 94–97
Termites of 1938, 33, 112
They Stooge to Conga, 43,
   55, 65, 115
Three Arabian Nuts, 119
Three Dark Horses, 120
Three-dimensional movies, 94
Three Dumb Clucks, 90, 112
Three Hams on Rye, 119
Three Little Beers, 111
Three Little Pigskins, 41, 44,
   65, 110
Three Little Pirates, 117
Three Little Sew and Sews,
   45, 112
Three Little Twirps, 115
Three Loan Wolves, 116
Three Missing Links, 112
Three Pests in a Mess, 116
Three Sappy People, 66, 113
Three Smart Saps, 114
Three Stooges, creation of, 1
Three Stooges Club, 103
Three Stooges comic book
   series, 94, 98
Three Stooges Go Around the
   World in a Daze, 24, 108
Three Stooges impersonators,
   46–47

Three Stooges in King
   Arthur's Court, The, 89
Three Stooges in Orbit, The,
   24, 89, 97, 108
Three Stooges Meet Hercules,
   The, 24, 108
Three Stooges Meet the
   Space Men, The, 89
Three Stooges Scrapbook,
   The, 97, 99
Three Stooges–themed
   products, 102–3
Three Troubledoers, The, 116
Thurston, Howard, 16
Time Out for Rhythm, 109
Tooth Will Out, The, 67, 119
Tricky Dicks, 92, 120
Triple Crossed, 93, 123
Triple slap, 78, illus. 78
Tuneophobia, 59
Turn Back the Clock, 108

U

Ullman, Elwood, 22–24, 89
Uncivil Warbirds, 116
Uncivil Warriors, 111
"Uncle Phineas," 38
Up in Daisy's Penthouse, 90,
   120
Use of old footage, 89–90

V

Vagabond Loafers, 63, 65, 90,
   118
Violent Is the Word for Curly,
   60, 65, 112

W

Walker, Sid, 29
Walsh, Jack, 31, illus. 32

Wardell, Joseph, 16
Warren, Lou, 28–29
Wax Museum, 27
We Want Our Mummy, 112
Wee Wee Monsieur, 112
Welker, Frank, 102
Wham-Bam-Slam, 92, 121
What's the Matador?, 93, 114
White, Jules, 8, 19–20, 89, 94, 112–23, *illus.* 19
Who Done It?, 44, 92, 118
Whoops I'm an Indian, 33, 111
Winchell, Paul, 102

Wolf, Jack, 29, 31
Wolf, Warner, 29
Woman Haters, 22, 33, 41, 86, 110
"Woo-Woo-Woo," origins of, 51–52

Y

Yes We Have No Bonanza, 66, 113
Yoke's on Me, The, 66, 115
You Nazty Spy, 113